JAMES DOUGLAS MERRITT is a New Englander who took his doctorate at the University of Wisconsin. His special fields of interest are nineteenth- and twentieth-century literature with an emphasis on Victorian poetry. He has published scholarly articles and has written a study of the twentieth-century English novelist Ronald Firbank that will be published in 1967. At present, Mr. Merritt is working on a study of the novels of Benjamin Disraeli and is an Assistant Professor of English at Brooklyn College.

The Pre-Raphaelite Poem

Edited, and with an introduction, by
James D. Merritt

New York/E. P. DUTTON & CO., INC./1966

The Pre-Raphaelite Poem

Dorothea Brooke married the learned Mr. Casaubon "when the Duke of Wellington was Prime Minister," and, as everyone knows, took a wedding trip to Rome with her new husband. The honeymoon was, of course, a failure for reasons that are of no concern here, but the dreariness of those days was briefly relieved when Dorothea sat to a young German artist who wished to use her as a model for Santa Clara. He was Adolf Naumann who "was one of the chief renovators of Christian art, one of those who had not only revived but expanded that grand conception of supreme events as mysteries at which the successive ages were spectators, and in relation to which the great souls of all periods became as it were contemporaries." [1] This estimate of Naumann's importance came from Will Ladislaw, who was not always as rational in Dorothea's presence as he might have been, and should not be taken as George Eliot's personal opinion. She had spoken, only a few pages earlier, of "certain long-haired German artists at Rome." in whom Romanticism "was fermenting . . . as a distinguishable enthusiasm" in which "the youth of other nations who worked or idled near them were sometimes caught." [2] Adolf Naumann and the "long haired German artists" were members of a group of painters known as the Nazarenes. Broadly speaking, the intention of the Nazarenes was, as Will Ladislaw said, to renovate Christian art and to make it more "truthful." Dorothea Brooke was not the only person from England to encounter them. Ford Maddox Brown saw the work of the Nazarenes in the 1840's, and he was to play a role

[1] George Eliot, *Middlemarch*, in *The Writings of George Eliot*, 25 vols. (Boston: 1908), XII, 309.

[2] *Ibid.*, p. 272.

in the Pre-Raphaelite movement, which was in many ways parallel to the Nazarenes. It started as a "Brotherhood" of earnest and intense young men, but it expanded until it became the widely known *avant-garde* of its day, and the foundation upon which the "Aesthetic" school of poetry and art would be built later in the century. The Pre-Raphaelites began with the intention of observing strict reality in their work, but only one of them, Millais, stayed with that intention, while the rest wrote poems and painted pictures that often contained elaborate and esoteric symbolism. The German Nazarenes in Rome were, as George Eliot says, infected with Romanticism, and so were the Pre-Raphaelites. The Nazarenes turned their efforts toward the renovation of Christian art; the Pre-Raphaelites turned their efforts toward the renovation of English art. Both groups rebelled against what their con-temporaries were doing, because it seemed imitative and old-fashioned, yet both ironically turned to even older schools of thought for their initial inspiration, and both groups withdrew from the nineteenth century in much of their work. The Pre-Raphaelites, partially as a result of their admiration for Keats, indulged in "neo-medievalism," which is to say that they rejected the realities of industrial Victorian England for the more picturesque haunts of a distant world unclouded by factory smoke or cinders spewing from railroad engines.

The definition of Pre-Raphaelitism has been a problem to everyone who has dealt with it.[3] Part of this problem, as William E. Fredeman has pointed out, has to do with establishing boundaries:

Critics and literary historians of the Victorian period have too often been inclined to denote only those aspects of Victorian romanticism centering on the Pre-Raphaelite Brother-

[3] For a discussion of some of these problems, see Howard Mumford Jones's "The Pre-Raphaelites" in *The Victorian Poets: A Guide to Research* (Cambridge, Mass., 1956).

hood. More accurately, the term includes three stages of a congeries of literary and artistic impulse which have been used loosely and interchangeably as synonymous: the Pre-Raphaelite Brotherhood, the Pre-Raphaelite Movement, and Pre-Raphaelitism. Actually, they are not mutually exclusive but sequential terms descriptive of a continuous, if not a unified, aesthetic force.[4]

The poetry that is "genuinely" Pre-Raphaelite must be that which appeared in the Pre-Raphaelite journal *The Germ*. Most of the poems from that journal are included in this collection, and may be seen as the "purest" literary products of the original Brotherhood and its closest affiliates. Yet *The Germ* died in the year of its birth, 1850, but the Pre-Raphaelite Movement continued and became the center of things for many artists and poets of the next two decades. Tennyson's "Maud," for example, especially the famous descriptive sections, is Pre-Raphaelite both in the time of its composition and in the images in which it abounds.

There are certain characteristics that may be seen as typical of all (or *almost* all) Pre-Raphaelite poetry:

1. A heavy use of descriptive detail.
2. Images that tend to be highly sensuous and full of color.
3. The occasional use of an obscure symbolism, such as repeated use of the number seven, and references to the more mysterious aspects of Christianity or of "pagan" religions.
4. A tendency to lend the tone (if not the form) of a ballad to the narrative.
5. The frequent use of subjects that have an innate

[4] William E. Fredeman, *Pre-Raphaelitism: A Bibliocritical Study* (Cambridge, Mass., 1965), p. 1. Mr. Fredeman's book is not only a massive compilation and bibliography on all aspects of the movement; it is also full of sound judgments. To one seriously interested in Pre-Raphaelitism beyond the realms of an anthology, it is the one indispensable book.

poignancy or morbidity. Many of these subjects were taken from literary sources.

6. Deliberate "medievalism," such as the use of vaguely medieval-sounding words, or the use of settings that, though unidentified, seem pre-Renaissance.

The Pre-Raphaelites' use of descriptive detail is one of the hallmarks of their work; sometimes these details seem to be applied to a thin framework and to be the *raison d'être* for the poem. The abundant use of such detail is the chief reason for the great length of many Pre-Raphaelite poems. It may be said that this detail is often used when it is not necessarily relevant to the narrative. The images by which most of this detail is presented are sensual, and may be seen as deriving from the example of Keats. There is this difference, however, that Keats often injects himself into the image, as in the "Ode to a Nightingale" where it is he who wishes for the "beaker full of the warm south." In the Pre-Raphaelite poems, the sensual imagery is used to decorate an idea or story about someone who could not possibly be the poet himself. Only in Dante Gabriel Rossetti's sonnets from *The House of Life* and in some of Christina Rossetti's lyrics does one sense a deep personal involvement such as that which characterized Romantic poetry earlier in the century. The Pre-Raphaelites are, in short, largely believers in "art for art's sake"; that phrase, with all its pejorative overtones, should be taken as a literal description of the purpose behind the poems, rather than as one that attempts to force the Pre-Raphaelites into the "Aesthetic" mold.

The symbols of the Pre-Raphaelites are, like those in some of their paintings, not always clear in reference. They are generally "mysterious" in that they seem to imply some association with things supernatural—that is, they do not, like most modern symbols, refer to abstractions such as "the meaninglessness of life" or the "hypocrisy of the middle class." They tend to be "Christian," except in Swinburne, where they are "pagan."

Of the ballad tone in many of the poems, one must be immediately aware. The language is often simple, and the presentation of the narrative is simple; events of widely varying degrees of importance are treated in the same tone of voice within a single poem. In many of the longer narratives there are disclosures (in the sense of plot disclosures) as the poem progresses. There is often a refrain employed that further heightens the impression that one is reading a ballad. Finally, the ballad tone is set by the fact that many of the narratives deal with extremely complex passions and motives, such as love, hate, or revenge, in a simple way, so that there is an immediacy about the story that is characteristic of the ballad.

Death is the central theme of many of the poems in *The Germ*, while there are poignant overtones in almost every poem by members of the movement. D. G. Rossetti's "Blessed Damozel," for example, waits for her lover in heaven. She is lonely and full of longing. Her lover on earth "hears" her tears. This love of melancholy things is another mark of the Pre-Raphaelites' affinity with Romanticism, as is their interest in things medieval.

There are differences between the Pre-Raphaelite Romantics and those of Keats's era, however. Their poems do not lay bare the soul of the poet, as do those of the earlier Romantics. They avoid, too, the moral or philosophical guidance that the poetry of most of their Victorian contemporaries offered. Their poems may be seen as the next step in English Romanticism, the step beyond the work of the first, great Romantics such as Wordsworth, Coleridge, and Keats. They are, in a sense, "Decadent" Romantics, just as the "Aestheticism" of the Nineties is, in a sense, "Decadent" Pre-Raphaelitism.

The Pre-Raphaelites have suffered the fate of all once *avant-garde* movements, the eventual decline in reputation that results from the appearance of a newer *avant-garde*. The twentieth century has been particularly contemptuous of their work, and it has been only in the last decade that scholarly interest in them has seriously revived, while general popular approval is still spotty. The reaction against them is natural, for their influence by the end of the nineteenth century was all-pervading enough to beget imitations of their style in such diverse places as a fountain in front of the Carnegie Library in Pittsburgh, and murals in the lobby of the Library of Congress, to name only two of many, many examples. Thousands of stained-glass windows in turn-of-the-century houses and churches depict Pre-Raphaelite ladies or saints, and thousands of prints of Rossetti's *Annunciation* doubtlessly still exist in attics, if not actually in genteel living rooms. These imitations and reproductions are the products of the "Decadent" or mannerist phase of Pre-Raphaelitism, just as the "shocking" poems of the Aesthetes are the product of the "Decadent" period in Pre-Raphaelite literature.

What can be clearly seen in any review of Pre-Raphaelite painting and poetry is that it is one of the unique movements in European art in that it was both distinctly literary and distinctly graphic at the same time. Most of the painters wrote poetry, and most of the poets painted pictures. Several, such as Dante Gabriel Rossetti and William Morris, wrote poetry, painted pictures, and were designers as well. Rossetti designed book covers; Morris went further and established his own press, in which he handled all sides of book production. He also designed furniture and wallpaper and other household effects. Only in the novel and in music does one find a lack of serious Pre-Raphaelite involvement. Pre-Raphaelite taste touched upon almost every aspect of artistic life in England, however, and when Gilbert and Sullivan produced *Patience* in 1881, it was far more than Oscar Wilde that they referred to when their Aesthetic hero, Bunthorne, offered this advice to the audience:

Be eloquent in praise of the very dull old days which have
　　long since passed away,
And convince 'em, if you can, that the reign of good Queen
　　Anne was Culture's palmiest day.
Of course you will pooh-pooh, whatever's fresh and new, and
　　declare it's crude and mean,
For art stopped short in the cultivated court of the
　　Empress Josephine.

Then a sentimental passion of a vegetable fashion must
　　excite your languid spleen,
An attachment à la Plato for a bashful young potato, or
　　a not-too-French French bean!
Though the Philistines may jostle, you will rank as an
　　Apostle in the high Aesthetic band, 　,
If you walk down Piccadilly with a poppy or a lily in your
　　medieval hand.

Things had gone too far by 1880, and what began as a Brotherhood of highly serious painters had degenerated into the extremes of the *fin de siècle*. Dante Gabriel Rossetti died in 1882, and one may take that year as the one in which Pre-Raphaelitism, as a distinct and viable "school," died too.

THE FOUNDING OF THE P.R.B.

At the end of the 1840's in England, the art of painting seemed to be in decline. Sir Joshua Reynolds and Gainsborough had both been dead for more than half a century, and even Constable had been dead for a decade. To many observers it seemed that there was little new talent coming along to take the place of the vanished giants. The Royal Academy, where Raphael and other masters of the High Renaissance were still held to be the standards by which all art should be judged, was not producing men to add vitality to the artistic life of Britain. In 1848 the art critic of the influential *Athenaeum* noted that "portraiture was a department which is rapidly falling into disrepute," and suggested that this was due to the fact that artists were making only a "small attempt to evoke character from the representation of human physiognomy." Portraiture had been one of the glories of English painting in the days of Sir Joshua, and now it was enfeebled. In landscape painting the situation was little better; Edwin Landseer (who was soon to become Sir Edwin, thanks to the pleasure Queen Victoria took in his work) dominated the scene, although his pictures contained little that was original and much that was merely superficially "pretty." There was, in short, a vacuum waiting to be filled.

Dante Gabriel Rossetti, William Holman Hunt, and John Everett Millais, none of whom was over twenty-one, were talented, original, and rebellious, and they had ideas about the "truth" of art, and especially about truthful representation of the subject. The beautiful madonnas and gloriously martyred saints depicted in the canvases of Raphael and other High Renaissance painters seemed to them to have nothing to do with the "truth" of motherhood or martyrdom, while the beautiful gardens and landscapes in which the subject was usually shown were idealizations rather than realities. They were, therefore, anti-Raphael. When they came across a book of engravings of some frescoes in the Campo Santo in Pisa, frescoes done in a naturalistic manner by painters who predated Raphael, their enthusiasm for change found a focus, and Pre-Raphaelitism was born or, at least, it was conceived, for the masters of the Campo Santo frescoes were not to be used as models in the way in which Raphael had been used for a model by the academicians. Instead, the earlier masters would serve as an inspiration for a new naturalism, a return to painting that depicted the subject realistically.

Thus the three young artists called themselves the Pre-Raphaelite Brotherhood, although to the public they were to be known at first only by the mysterious initials "P.R.B."

From the moment that it became known, the P.R.B. was the center of a stormy aesthetic argument that eventually included such diverse figures on the Victorian scene as Ruskin (who was the first important person to defend it) and Charles Dickens (whose vicious attack upon Millais's *Christ in the House of His Parents*—he found it "mean, odious, repulsive, and revolting"—represents the horror aroused in polite breasts by the new realism). Due, no doubt, to their notoriety, the original members of the P.R.B. found that they had supporters among the younger poets and painters of the period, and the founding trio was expanded to include James Collinson, Frederic George Stephens, and Dante Gabriel Rossetti's brother, William. It was not long before any vestiges of the Brotherhood had disappeared, and the movement, for such it might now be called, came to include Ford Maddox Brown (who brought word of the "Nazarenes" from Rome), Edward Burne-Jones, Coventry Patmore, Algernon Charles Swinburne, Simeon Solomon, and Christina Rossetti. Poetry took its place beside painting as one of the chief modes of expression of Pre-Raphaelite ideas.

Although the Brotherhood had ceased to exist, the initials "P.R.B." lingered on and served as an object of scorn and the subject of wits, one of whom, upon hearing that these letters were to be carved upon the nameplate for a studio door suggested that they would be taken to mean "Please Ring Bell." Not all the jokes were as kind (or as successful), and much of the criticism was vicious. Millais's *Christ in the House of His Parents*, for instance, was subjected to some remarkably nasty criticism. It showed Jesus in Joseph's carpentry shop (the model for Joseph was "a real carpenter") surrounded by members of the Holy Family. The child has wounded his hand upon a nail and a drop of blood has fallen onto his foot—obviously, Millais is symbolically foreshadowing the wounds of the Crucifixion. A critic in *Blackwood's Magazine*, however, could see little but "a collection of splay feet, puffed joints, and misshapen limbs." *The Times* shudderingly observed that "Mr. Millais's . . . picture is, to speak plainly, revolting." It was the "loathesome minuteness" which most offended the critics. It seemed a serious affront against propriety to depict Joseph as an ordinary man (with ugly feet and not very clean hands) or to show Jesus as an ordinary little boy in a highly realistic carpenter's shop. Yet the symbolism is there too, for in addition to the wounds, one may see sheep through an open door that represent the souls to be saved by the sacrifice of the shepherd Jesus. The public was not ready for the sort of thing the Pre-Raphaelites were attempting to do.

One wonders today what could have caused such a fuss. The draftsmanship of Millais's picture is very good, while the use of color and detail in the works of his fellow Pre-Raphaelites commands admiration for artists who took their work so seriously. Sometimes, perhaps, they took their realism too seriously, with results that tended toward the bizarre. When he was painting his *Ophelia*, for example, Millais asked his model to pose under remarkably difficult circumstances. Ophelia was to be shown floating in the river, singing her "melodious lay" only moments before "her garments, heavy with their drink," pulled her "to muddy death." The model was Elizabeth Siddal (who later married Dante Gabriel Rossetti); perhaps it is best to tell the story in the words of Millais's son:

Miss Siddal had a trying experience whilst acting as a model for "Ophelia." In order that the artist might get the proper set of the garments in water and the right atmosphere and aqueous effects, she had to lie in a large bath filled with water, which was kept at an even temperature by lamps placed beneath. One day, just as the picture was nearly finished, the lamps went out unnoticed by the artist, who was so intensely absorbed in his work that he thought of nothing else, and the poor lady was kept floating in the cold water till she was quite benumbed. She herself never complained of this, but the result was that she contracted a severe cold, and her father (an auctioneer at Oxford) wrote to Millais, threatening him with an action for £50 damages for his carelessness. Eventually the matter was satisfactorily compromised. Millais paid the doctor's bill; and Miss Siddal, quickly recovering, was none the worse for her cold bath.[5]

The painting that resulted from Elizabeth Siddal's "trying experience" is one of the most beautiful produced by the Pre-Raphaelites. It is remarkably minute in its detail, not only the detail of Ophelia's waterlogged gown, but the detail of the grass and weeds along the riverbank is also very fine; Millais sat by a riverbank for days, half eaten by flies and gnats, until he had exactly reproduced everything he saw. Like the other members of the movement, he was a craftsman who took his work very seriously. The same craftsmanship is evident in the poems of his Pre-Raphaelite brethren.

The Germ: 1850

All this talk about painting would seem to have little to do with poetry, but in fact it is highly relevant. In 1849, only a year after the establishment of the P.R.B., William Michael Rossetti said of one of his verses that "the informing idea of the poem was to apply to versewriting the same principles of strict actuality and probability of detail which the Pre-Raphaelites upheld in their

[5] John Guille Millais, *The Life and Letters of Sir John Everett Millais*, 2 vols. (New York: 1899), I, 144.

pictures."[6] His description of his own poem is not necessarily applicable to all Pre-Raphaelite poems, but it will serve as a starting point from which to discuss the contents of *The Germ*, for the "strict actuality" that Millais sought when he put Miss Siddal in a bathtub is something like that which underlies William Michael's own poems in the journal, as well as those of several other poets included in it.

The Germ lived a precarious existence for four months during 1850. Numbers 1 and 2 were published in January and February of that year, while numbers 3 and 4 appeared during the next two months under the new title, *Art and Poetry, Being Thoughts Towards Nature, Conducted Principally by Artists*. The journal was by no means a success financially, but it presented the Pre-Raphaelite case with vigor. Some thought it unwholesome, but one nineteenth-century critic defended it in this way:

> The magazine was written by men for men, and not for school misses in simpers and curl papers. It was frank and bold, but *unwholesomeness* existed only in the mind of him who went to seek it. Prophetic in its title, it was before its time; its aims were not understood; the circle to which it appealed was too small; but *The Germ* was there whence a great and beautiful tree has grown up.[7]

The frankness and boldness of the magazine do not seem striking to a contemporary reader, but perhaps that is partially due to the fact that *The Germ did* manage to exist for four months in the middle of the nineteenth century.

Whether or not one accepts such a bald statement about the importance of *The Germ*, the fact is that it did deal with painting and poetry as companion arts, and it

[6] Quoted in Ford Maddox Hueffer (later, Ford Maddox Ford), *The Pre-Raphaelite Brotherhood* (London: 1907), p. 98.

[7] Walter Hamilton, *The Aesthetic Movement in England*, 2nd ed. (London: 1882), pp. 11–12.

treated these arts with a seriousness that commands attention. William Michael Rossetti composed a sonnet for the wrappers of *The Germ* that pleasantly states the case:

> When whoso merely hath a little thought
>   Will plainly think the thought which is in him,
> Not imagining another's, bright or dim,
>   Not mangling with new words that others thought;
> When whoso speaks, from having either sought
>   Or only found—will speak, not just to skim
> A shallow surface with words made and trim,
>   But in that very speech the matter brought:
> Be not too keen to cry—"So this is all!
>   "A thing I might myself have thought as well,
> "But would not say it, for it was not worth!"
>   Ask, "Is this truth?" For is it still to tell
> That, be the theme a point, or the whole earth,
>   Truth is a circle, perfect, great or small?

The perfect "circle" that is truth may be open to a million interpretations, but the Pre-Raphaelites' idealistic concern with it is the central theme of *The Germ*. Other and later movements in art were to think that a manifesto was important; while *The Germ* is not a genuine manifesto in that it does not outline the purposes of the movement in a few neat sentences, it is a very early example of what might be called manifesto-making in art.

Some of the prose pieces in *The Germ* have a fairly windy tone about them, an *ex cathedra* tone that is unbecoming to the youth of the writers, but it would be impossible to find anything comparable to these views on art, *by artists*, in Victorian England.

The poems vary in style and subject matter from those of William Michael Rossetti's "Fancies at Leisure" (several of which are remarkably similar to some of the Imagist poems of the twentieth century), to those of his sister, Christina, which contain some of the enthusiasm of the Evangelical movement. Coventry Patmore (who ceased to be a Pre-Raphaelite shortly after the publication of *The Germ*) contributed uxorious fancies, and James Collinson produced a very long poem (part of which is included on pages 181-184) upon the early life of Jesus in which events from the adult life of Christ are foreshadowed in the childish occurrences in the home of his parents—it is, obviously, similar to Millais's painting on the same subject. Dante Gabriel Rossetti, whose name is the one most closely associated with Pre-Raphaelitism in the minds of most people, produced "The Blessed Damozel," which is full of the sensual imagery typical of the movement, and others, including a description of the carillons at Bruges and Antwerp. *The Germ* also contains his "Sonnets for Pictures" in which he describes and comments upon the work of other artists—another indication of the close relationship between painting and poetry in the eyes of the Pre-Raphaelites.

Although these poems are varied in mood and subject, they all share to some extent the common concern of attempting to present reality. Collinson's "Child Jesus" shows us a very human child, and William Michael Rossetti is meticulous in presenting scenic details. Even Christina Rossetti's most fervently religious poems (such as "Repining," page 94) have images that are realistic. The motivating purpose of these poems was the desire for "strict actuality" that William Michael Rossetti had mentioned, and it is usually there, though occasionally the subject (again, Christina Rossetti's "Repining" is an example) forces the poet to extend his images until they are surrealistic. Pre-Raphaelite poems published after 1850 regularly stray from reality, as in Christina Rossetti's "Goblin Market" (page 71) with its images of the weird little tempters who seem like creatures out of an Hieronymous Bosch painting, or in Swinburne's "pagan" poems with their vague symbolism and allusions to earth-mother goddesses. Dante Gabriel Rossetti's poems, sometimes influenced by his lifelong admiration for and study of Dante Alighieri, often stray into the realm of surrealism, as in the "Willowwood" sonnets from *The House of Life* (see page 55). But this is getting a bit ahead of *The Germ*, the demise of which did *not* signal a decline in Pre-Raphaelite influence or success.

RUSKIN AND THE SPREAD OF PRE-RAPHAELITISM

John Ruskin, the most important art critic of Victorian England, came to the defense of the Pre-Raphaelites in the columns of *The Times* in May, 1851. He had already written about "truth" in art, and he recognized in them practitioners of the principles he had already proposed. That is not to say that the P.R.B. owed its formation to Ruskin's writings; it did not, and Ruskin never laid claim to that achievement.

Ruskin's defense set off attacks upon himself as well as continued attacks upon the Pre-Raphaelites, yet it was his voice that did much to lend a degree of respectability to the movement and to make it an important force in English art. As evidence of this new importance, Pre-Raphaelite painters were chosen to do the frescoes for the new Oxford Union, and Oxford, after all, was one of the seats of the English Establishment. Unfortunately, the frescoes were never finished (they were begun in 1857), and the work that was completed disintegrated because the painters did not make sure that the walls were suitably prepared for frescoes. Yet exhibitions in London and New York spread their fame further afield, and when Moxon published an edition of Tennyson's *Poems* in 1857, Hunt, Millais, and Rossetti provided illustrations, an irrefutable indication that in less than ten years the members of the P.R.B. had achieved respectability.

A number of less well-known poets came to be associated with the Pre-Raphaelites, such as Arthur O'Shaugh-

nessy, John Payne, William Allingham, and Philip Bourke
Marston (all of whom are represented in this collection),
while the poetry of Dante Gabriel and Christina Rossetti
was earning a broad reputation. In 1861 Rossetti pub-
lished his translations of early Italian poets and Dante's
Vita Nuova, which extended the boundaries of the Pre-
Raphaelite movement as well as adding to its distinction.
Christina Rossetti's "Goblin Market" with its strangely
Skeltonic verses and its brilliant images, was published in
1862, and was widely read.

William Morris had fallen under the influence of Rossetti, and published *The Defence of Guenevere and Other
Poems* in 1858 (see page 122). It "is in many respects the
most Pre-Raphaelite volume of poetry which the movement produced,"[8] and by so doing Morris added Arthurian
legend to the subject matter of Pre-Raphaelite poetry.
Although Morris was to quarrel with Rossetti later, the
motivating force in his early work was Pre-Raphaelite, and
his work continued to show that influence even when he
had moved into his later phase and become interested in
such things as the Nibelung legends. The pictorial quality
typical of the movement never left his poetry.

COMIC RELIEF: "THE FLESHLY SCHOOL OF POETRY"

Although the history of the Pre-Raphaelite movement
up to this point seems to be one of reassuring progress
and growing public acceptance, there were critical snipers
waiting in the bushes. Algernon Charles Swinburne was
to be the first target in a minor skirmish that quickly
spread into a major literary war of nearly ten-years'
duration.

Swinburne had come under Pre-Raphaelite influence
while still an undergraduate at Oxford. When he published his *Poems and Ballads* in 1866, the "paganism" of

[8] Fredeman, *op. cit.*, p. 162.

many of the poems (see "Hertha," for example, page 163) shocked the philistines. The critic of the *Saturday Review* was so appalled that he dubbed him the "libidinous laureate of a pack of satyrs." Swinburne was hot tempered, and when he found himself among those satirized in anonymous verses published in the *Spectator*, the battle began. The *Spectator* verses were actually written by Robert Buchanan, a minor critic and poet from Scotland who was to play a central role in the whole affair. Buchanan's satire was titled "The Session of the Poets," and it made fun of many poets, including Tennyson, Browning, and Arnold. The Swinburne stanza is as follows:

What was said? what was done? was there prosing or rhyming?
   Was nothing noteworthy in deed or in word?
Why, just as the hour for the supper was chiming,
   The only event of the evening occurred.

Up jumped, with his neck stretching out like a gander,
   Master Swinburne, and squeal'd, glaring out through his
     hair,
'All Virtue is bosh! Hallelujah for Landor.
   I disbelieve wholly in everything!—there!'

The number of combatants was expanded when William Michael Rossetti came to Swinburne's defense with an essay that praised *Poems and Ballads* and referred to Buchanan as a troublemaker.

Dante Gabriel Rossetti was brought into the matter in 1870 when he published his *Poems*, which led the injudicious Buchanan to write his famous article for the *Contemporary Review*, "The Fleshly School of Poetry." In it he charged that Rossetti, along with Swinburne and William Morris, had formed "a solemn league and covenant to extol fleshliness as the distinct and supreme end of poetic and pictorial art." The article appeared over the name "Thomas Maitland," but the fact of Buchanan's authorship was soon known, and Rossetti prepared an enraged reply that his lawyers persuaded him to destroy; he finally contented himself with a more discreet response bearing the witty title "The Stealthy School of Criticism." He denied the "solemn league . . . to extol fleshliness" but added:

That I may, nevertheless, take a wider view than some poets or critics, of how much, in the material conditions absolutely given to man to deal with as distinct from his spiritual aspirations, is admissable within the limits of art—this, I say, is possible enough; nor do I wish to shrink from such responsibility. But to state that I do so to the ignoring or overshadowing of spiritual beauty, is an absolute falsehood, impossible to put forward except in the indulgence of prejudice or rancour.

Rossetti was well known by this time and was, in fact, one of the most respected of living poets. Buchanan was witless enough to keep the issue before the public by expanding his original "Fleshly School of Poetry" essay into a pamphlet published in 1872.

Swinburne re-entered; he attacked Buchanan in a satirical piece titled "Under the Microscope." Buchanan returned the attack in "The Monkey and the Microscope." The war had been going on for well over five years by this time, but it was to continue for nearly four more. In 1875, *Jonas Fisher*, "consisting of about 240 pages of the most dismal, dreary doggerel that ever was written," [9] was published anonymously. It was, in fact, by James Carnegie, the Earl of Southesk, but Swinburne attributed it to Buchanan, and assumed himself to be the object of scorn in the following stanzas:

> I am one of those who howl
>   Whene'er the smallest word is said,
> That might not fittingly appeal
>   In books to little children read.

[9] The judgment is that of Walter Hamilton, *op. cit.*, p. 65.

> Nor do I shudder over-much
> (However little I approve),
> When men like Byron sing too free
> Of downright, honest, man-like love.
>
> But what my very soul abhors,
> What almost turns my blood to bile,
> Is when some prurient paganist
> Stands up, and warbles with a smile,
>
> A sick, putrescent, dulcet lay,
> Like sugared sauce with meat too high,
> To hymn, or hint, the sensuous charms
> Of morbid immorality.[10]

He replied in "The Devil's Due," which *he* signed "Thomas Maitland," and described Buchanan as the "multifaced idyllist of the gutter." For once, Buchanan was innocent, at least of the ridiculous *Jonas Fisher*, and he sued Swinburne for £5,000 damages. The trial was much enjoyed by the public. The defense pointed out that Buchanan had little right to set himself up as the guardian of English morals against "fleshliness" when he had written such lines as these:

> Till with passionate sensation,
> Body and brain began to burn,
> And he yielded to the bursting,
> Burning, blinding, hungering, thirsting
> Passion felt by beasts and men!
> And his eyes caught love and rapture,
> And he held her close in capture,
> Kissing lips that kiss'd again.[11]

It was really little more than mud-slinging when Swinburne's lawyer told the jury:

. . . in one poem [of Buchanan's], I find a coster girl, who lived in the neighbourhood of St. Giles's, and fell into diffi-

[10] Quoted by Hamilton, *op. cit.*, p. 66.
[11] *Ibid.*, pp. 69–70.

culty with a gentleman, who himself pursued a course of life which ultimately brought him to the gallows. Another poem is entitled "Liz." Here is the life of a wretchedly poor girl, who has been seduced by one of the low persons who inhabit the same classical locality I have already mentioned, and who has got an illegitimate child. These are the stories in which Mr. Robert Buchanan delights. He has written under various names, and has libeled other people. He has used hard words . . . and, considering things that he had written himself, he could hardly complain if some people thought it fit also to pull them to pieces.[12]

Buchanan won his case, although he was awarded only £150 instead of £5,000. The money must have been cold comfort, however, for along with it he earned the scorn of the whole Pre-Raphaelite band as well as of the responsible critics and scholars of the time. The Pre-Raphaelites lost the battle but they won the war.

Rossetti's friends suggested that his last years were shortened because of Buchanan's attack, but the charge is probably no more defensible than that which attributed the death of Keats to unfavorable reviews of *his* poetry. Buchanan tried to undo some of the damage, going so far as to say that "fleshly" love was "the highest human pleasure." It was much too late, and Buchanan sank into obscurity except as the author of the absurd and infamous "Fleshly School of Poetry" controversy. It was a richly deserved fate.

PRE-RAPHAELITISM, AESTHETICISM, AND THE FIN DE SIÈCLE

First, and above all other considerations, the leaders of the Aesthetic School in poetry have been styled fleshly poets, delighting in somewhat sensually-suggestive descriptions of the passions, ornamented with hyperbolical metaphor, or told in curious archaic speech; and dressed up in quaint medieval garments of odd old ballad rhymes and phrases.

[12] *Ibid.*, pp. 70–71.

The strict *Aesthete* admires only what in his language is known as *intense*. . . . Henry Irving, the actor, is undeniably *intense*, and they worship him; indeed, one fair votary of the sunflower goddess was heard to remark that his left leg was a poem in itself. . . . In music the Aesthetes affect Liszt, Rubenstein, and Wagner, who are all most consummately intense. . . . In painting the Aesthetes have a great veneration for Allessandro Botticelli, a Florentine artist, who flourished about four centuries ago. . . . In architecture the Queen Anne style is favoured. . . . Chippendale furniture, dados, old-fashioned brass and wrought iron work, medieval lamps, stained glass in small squares, and old china are all held to be the outward and visible signs of an inward and spiritual grace and intensity.[13]

This description of Aestheticism and the tastes of the Aesthetes is very mildly tongue-in-cheek, but its main purpose was, according to its author, to acquaint the English public with the then new movement in art. It was not intended to present the Aesthetes as ridiculous, which *had* been the intention of Gilbert and Sullivan in their production of *Patience*, which was playing in London when these words were written. It is obvious that Pre-Raphaelite tastes and Aesthetic tastes were in many ways similar; certainly the intensity that is seen as the distinguishing mark of Aestheticism is evident in much of the work of the Pre-Raphaelites.

We have already noted that art for its own sake was a prime concern of the Pre-Raphaelites (although they didn't state it as baldly as the Aesthetes did), but they tended to deplore the merely precious and, of course, emphasized the realistic. When they spoke about the "truth" of art, they meant the degree to which art literally represented life (life as *they* saw it), whereas the Aesthetes were likelier to hold with Oscar Wilde's declaration that life imitates art, rather than the reverse.

[13] Hamilton, *op. cit.*, pp. 31–34.

The enthusiasms of the Pre-Raphaelites, the earnestness that marks so much of their work, was metamorphosed later in the century into the posturing and posing of the Aesthetes, while the realism that they attempted to reproduce tended toward a kind of "shock-the-bourgeois" abandon in the Aesthetes. Though Aestheticism often seems to be Pre-Raphaelitism gone slightly mad, the two movements are inextricably bound together, and it is extremely unlikely that Aestheticism would have developed at all if the P.R.B. had not been founded in 1848.

Describing himself in an early volume of his *Autobiographies*, William Butler Yeats said of himself as a young man, "I was in all things Pre-Raphaelite."[14] Thus the greatest poet of the twentieth century acknowledged his debt to a movement that at first glance seems to have been eons removed from his own, later symbolist poetry. Yet even in the great poems written after he had attempted to withdraw himself from his earlier Romanticism (such as "Sailing to Byzantium") one often finds the vivid, pictorial images, the heavy use of color images, and the desire to escape from the world of "dying generations" into a world of art; the method may be different from that of the Pre-Raphaelites, but the prevailing tone and theme are much the same.

It may be said that when the great Romantic movement in English poetry seemed to be at an end at the death of Keats, it was given new life by the founding of the Pre-Raphaelite Brotherhood at mid-century. Thus one of the richest movements in English poetry was extended and expanded. When Pre-Raphaelitism itself declined into the jaded tastes of the *fin de siècle*, the great imaginative force of Romanticism that had been the seemingly endless source of English poetry for a century diminished until it

[14] William Butler Yeats, *Autobiographies: Reveries Over Childhood and Youth and The Trembling of the Veil* (New York: 1927), p. 141.

nearly ceased to exist. New and vital poetic movements were to replace it, but Pre-Raphaelitism remains as one of the spots of bright color in Victorian England, and its existence made possible the freedom that is the basis of contemporary poetry.

JAMES D. MERRITT

University of Pittsburgh
Pittsburgh, Pennsylvania

THE BLESSED DAMOZEL *

The blessed damozel leaned out
  From the gold bar of heaven;
Her eyes were deeper than the depth
  Of water stilled at even;
She had three lilies in her hand,
  And the stars in her hair were seven.

Her robe, ungirt from clasp to hem,
  No wrought flowers did adorn,
But a white rose of Mary's gift,
  For service meetly worn;   10
Her hair that lay along her back
  Was yellow like ripe corn.

Herseemed she scarce had been a day
  One of God's choristers;
The wonder was not yet quite gone
  From that still look of hers;
Albeit, to them she left, her day
  Had counted as ten years.

(To *one* it is ten years of years.
  . . . Yet now, and in this place,   20
Surely she leaned o'er me—her hair
  Fell all about my face. . . .
Nothing: the autumn fall of leaves.
  The whole year sets apace.)

It was the rampart of God's house
  That she was standing on;
By God built over the sheer depth
  The which is Space begun;

  * Published in *The Germ*.

So high, that looking downward thence
    She scarce could see the sun. 30

It lies in heaven, across the flood
    Of ether, as a bridge.
Beneath the tides of day and night
    With flame and darkness ridge
The void, as low as where this earth
    Spins like a fretful midge.

Around her, lovers, newly met
    'Mid deathless love's acclaims,
Spoke evermore among themselves
    Their heart-remembered names; 40
And the souls mounting up to God
    Went by her like thin flames.

And still she bowed herself and stooped
    Out of the circling charm;
Until her bosom must have made
    The bar she leaned on warm,
And the lilies lay as if asleep
    Along her bended arm.

From the fixed place of heaven she saw
    Time like a pulse shake fierce 50
Through all the worlds. Her gaze still strove
    Within the gulf to pierce
Its path; and now she spoke as when
    The stars sang in their spheres.

The sun was gone now; the curled moon
    Was like a little feather
Fluttering far down the gulf; and now
    She spoke through the still weather.
Her voice was like the voice the stars
    Had when they sang together. 60

(Ah, sweet! Even now, in that bird's song,
    Strove not her accents there,

34/*Dante Gabriel Rossetti*

Fain to be harkened? When those bells
   Possessed the mid-day air,
Strove not her steps to reach my side
   Down all the echoing stair?)

"I wish that he were come to me,
   For he will come," she said.
"Have I not prayed in heaven?—on earth,
   Lord, Lord, has he not prayed?   70
Are not two prayers a perfect strength?
   And shall I feel afraid?

"When round his head the aureole clings,
   And he is clothed in white,
I'll take his hand and go with him
   To the deep wells of light;
As unto a stream we will step down,
   And bathe there in God's sight.

"We two will stand beside that shrine,
   Occult, withheld, untrod,   80
Whose lamps are stirred continually
   With prayers sent up to God;
And see our old prayers, granted, melt
   Each like a little cloud.

"We two will lie i' the shadow of
   That living mystic tree
Within whose secret growth the Dove
   Is sometimes felt to be,
While every leaf that His plumes touch
   Saith His Name audibly.   90

"And I myself will teach to him,
   I myself, lying so,
The songs I sing here; which his voice
   Shall pause in, hushed and slow,
And find some knowledge at each pause,
   Or some new thing to know."

(Alas! We two, we two, thou say'st!
   Yea, one wast thou with me
That once of old. But shall God lift
   To endless unity   100
The soul whose likeness with thy soul
   Was but its love for thee?)

"We two," she said, "will seek the groves
   Where the lady Mary is,
With her five handmaidens, whose names
   Are five sweet symphonies,
Cecily, Gertrude, Magdalen,
   Margaret, and Rosalys.

"Circlewise sit they, with bound locks
   And foreheads garlanded;   110
Into the fine cloth white like flame
   Weaving the golden thread,
To fashion the birth-robes for them
   Who are just born, being dead.

"He shall fear, haply, and be dumb;
   Then will I lay my cheek
To his, and tell about our love,
   Not once abashed or weak;
And the dear Mother will approve
   My pride, and let me speak.   120

"Herself shall bring us, hand in hand,
   To Him round whom all souls
Kneel, the clear-ranged unnumbered heads
   Bowed with their aureoles;
And angels meeting us shall sing
   To their citherns and citoles.

"There will I ask of Christ the Lord
   Thus much for him and me—
Only to live as once on earth
   With Love, only to be,   130

As then awhile, forever now,
  Together, I and he."

She gazed and listened and then said,
  Less sad of speech than mild—
"All this is when he comes." She ceased.
  The light thrilled toward her, filled
With angels in strong, level flight.
  Her eyes prayed, and she smiled.

(I saw her smile.) But soon their path
  Was vague in distant spheres;   140
And then she cast her arms along
  The golden barriers,
And laid her face between her hands,
  And wept. (I heard her tears.)

SONNETS FOR PICTURES *

I

A VIRGIN AND CHILD, BY HANS MEMMELING; IN THE ACADEMY OF BRUGES

Mystery: God, Man's Life, born into man
  Of woman. There abideth on her brow
  The ended pang of knowledge, the which now
Is calm assured. Since first her task began,
She hath known all. What more of anguish than
  Endurance oft hath lived through, the whole space
  Through night till night, passed weak upon her face
While like a heavy flood the darkness ran?
All hath been told her touching her dear Son,
  And all shall be accomplished. Where he sits
    Even now, a babe, he holds the symbol fruit
Perfect and chosen. Until God permits,
  His soul's elect still have the absolute
Harsh nether darkness, and make painful moan.

* Published in *The Germ*.

II

Mystery: Katharine, the bride of Christ.
  She kneels, and on her hand the holy Child
  Setteth the ring. Her life is sad and mild,
Laid in God's knowledge—ever unenticed
From Him, and in the end thus fitly priced.
  Awe, and the music that is near her, wrought
  Of Angels, hath possessed her eyes in thought:
Her utter joy is her's, and hath sufficed.
There is a pause while Mary Virgin turns
    The leaf, and reads. With eyes on the spread book,
    That damsel at her knees reads after her.
    John whom He loved and John His harbinger
Listen and watch. Whereon soe'er thou look,
The light is starred in gems, and the gold burns.

III

(*It is necessary to mention, that this picture would appear
to have been in the artist's mind an allegory, which the modern spectator may seek vainly to interpret.*)

Scarcely, I think; yet it indeed *may* be
  The meaning reached him, when this music rang
  Sharp through his brain, a distinct rapid pang,
And he beheld these rocks and that ridg'd sea.
But I believe he just leaned passively,
  And felt their hair carried across his face
  As each nymph passed him; nor gave ear to trace
How many feet; nor bent assuredly
His eyes from the blind fixedness of thought
  To see the dancers. It is bitter glad
    Even unto tears. Its meaning filleth it,
    A portion of most secret life: to wit:—

Each human pulse shall keep the sense it had
With all, though the mind's labour run to nought.

IV

A VENETIAN PASTORAL, BY GIORGIONE; IN THE LOUVRE

(*In this picture, two cavaliers and an undraped woman are
seated in the grass, with musical instruments, while another
woman dips a vase into a well hard by, for water.*)

Water, for anguish of the solstice,—yea,
    Over the vessel's mouth still widening
    Listlessly dipt to let the water in
With slow vague gurgle. Blue, and deep away,
The heat lies silent at the brink of day.
    Now the hand trails upon the viol-string
    That sobs; and the brown faces cease to sing,
Mournful with complete pleasure. Her eyes stray
    In distance; through her lips the pipe doth creep
    And leaves them pouting; the green shadowed grass
        Is cool against her naked flesh. Let be:
Do not now speak unto her lest she weep,—
    Nor name this ever. Be it as it was:—
        Silence of heat, and solemn poetry.

V

"ANGELICA RESCUED FROM THE SEA-MONSTER," BY
INGRES; IN THE LUXEMBOURG

A remote sky, prolonged to the sea's brim:
    One rock-point standing buffetted alone,
    Vexed at its base with a foul beast unknown,
Hell-spurge of geomaunt and teraphim:
A knight, and a winged creature bearing him,
    Reared at the rock: a woman fettered there,
    Leaning into the hollow with loose hair
And throat let back and heartsick trail of limb.
The sky is harsh, and the sea shrewd and salt.
    Under his lord, the griffin-horse ramps blind

With rigid wings and tail. The spear's lithe stem
  Thrills in the roaring of those jaws: behind,
The evil length of body chafes at fault.
  She doth not hear nor see—she knows of them.

VI

THE SAME

Clench thine eyes now,—'tis the last instant, girl:
  Draw in thy senses, set thy knees, and take
  One breath for all: thy life is keen awake,—
Thou may'st not swoon. Was that the scattered whirl
Of its foam drenched thee?—or the waves that curl
  And split, bleak spray wherein thy temples ache?—
  Or was it his the champion's blood to flake
Thy flesh?—Or thine own blood's anointing, girl? . . . .
. . . . Now, silence: for the sea's is such a sound
  As irks not silence; and except the sea,
  All is now still. Now the dead thing doth cease
To writhe, and drifts. He turns to her: and she
Cast from the jaws of Death, remains there, bound,
  Again a woman in her nakedness.

SISTER HELEN

"Why did you melt your waxen man,
                Sister Helen?
Today is the third since you began."
"The time was long, yet the time ran,
                Little brother."
        (O Mother, Mary Mother,
Three days today, between Hell and Heaven!)

"But if you have done your work aright,
                Sister Helen,
You'll let me play, for you said I might." 10

"Be very still in your play tonight,
                    Little brother."
           (O Mother, Mary Mother,
Third night, tonight, between Hell and Heaven!)

"You said it must melt ere vesper-bell
                    Sister Helen;
If now it be molten, all is well."
"Even so—nay, peace! you cannot tell,
                    Little brother."
           (O Mother, Mary Mother,   20
O what is this, between Hell and Heaven?)

"Oh, the waxen knave was plump today,
                    Sister Helen;
How like dead folk he has dropped away!"
"Nay now, of the dead what can you say,
                    Little brother?"
           (O Mother, Mary Mother,
What of the dead, between Hell and Heaven?)

"See, see, the sunken pile of wood,
                    Sister Helen,   30
Shines through the thinned wax red as blood!"
"Nay now, when looked you yet on blood,
                    Little brother?"
           (O Mother, Mary Mother,
How pale she is, between Hell and Heaven!)

"Now close your eyes for they're sick and sore,
                    Sister Helen,
And I'll play without the gallery door."
"Aye, let me rest—I'll lie on the floor,
                    Little brother."   40
           (O Mother, Mary Mother,
What rest tonight between Hell and Heaven?)

"Here high up in the balcony,
                    Sister Helen,

The moon flies face to face with me."
"Aye, look and say whatever you see,
                    Little brother."
              (O Mother, Mary Mother,
What sight tonight, between Hell and Heaven?)

"Outside it's merry in the wind's wake,   50
                    Sister Helen;
In the shaken trees the chill stars shake."
"Hush, heard you a horse-tread as you spake,
                    Little brother?
              (O Mother, Mary Mother,
What sound tonight between Hell and Heaven?)

"I hear a horse-tread and I see,
                    Sister Helen,
Three horsemen that ride terribly."
"Little brother, whence come the three,   60
                    Little brother?"
              (O Mother, Mary Mother,
Whence should they come, between Hell and Heaven?)

"They come by the hill-verge from Boyne Bar,
                    Sister Helen,
And one draws nigh, but two are afar."
"Look, look, do you know them who they are,
                    Little brother?"
              (O Mother, Mary Mother,
Who should they be, between Hell and Heaven?)   70

"Oh, it's Keith of Eastholm rides so fast,
                    Sister Helen,
For I know the white mane on the blast."
"The hour has come, has come at last,
                    Little brother!"
              (O Mother, Mary Mother,
Her hour at last, between Hell and Heaven!)

"He has made a sign and called Halloo!

Sister Helen,
And he says that he would speak with you." 80
"Oh tell him I fear the frozen dew,
                    Little brother."
            (O Mother, Mary Mother,
Why laughs she thus, between Hell and Heaven?)

"The wind is loud, but I hear him cry,
                    Sister Helen,
That Keith of Ewern's like to die."
"And he and thou, and thou and I,
                    Little brother."
            (Oh Mother, Mary Mother, 90
And they and we, between Hell and Heaven!)

"Three days ago, on his marriage-morn,
                    Sister Helen,
He sickened, and lies since then forlorn."
"For bridegroom's side is the bride a thorn,
                    Little brother?"
            (O Mother, Mary Mother,
Cold bridal cheer, between Hell and Heaven!)

"Three days and nights he has lain abed,
                    Sister Helen, 100
And he prays in torment to be dead."
"The thing may chance, if he have prayed,
                    Little brother!"
            (O Mother, Mary Mother,
If he have prayed, between Hell and Heaven!)

"But he has not ceased to cry today,
                    Sister Helen,
That you should take your curse away."
"My prayer was heard—he need but pray,
                    Little brother!" 110
            (O Mother, Mary Mother,
Shall God not hear, between Hell and Heaven?)

"But he says, till you take back your ban,
                              Sister Helen,
His soul would pass, yet never can."
"Nay then, shall I slay a living man,
                              Little brother?"
              (O Mother, Mary Mother,
A *living* soul, between Hell and Heaven!)

"But he calls forever on your name,   120
                              Sister Helen,
And says that he melts before a flame."
"My heart for his pleasure fared the same,
                              Little brother,"
              (O Mother, Mary Mother,
Fire at the heart, between Hell and Heaven!)

"Here's Keith of Westholm riding fast,
                              Sister Helen,
For I know the white plume on the blast."
"The hour, the sweet hour I forecast,   130
                              Little brother!"
              (O Mother, Mary Mother,
Is the hour sweet, between Hell and Heaven?)

"He stops to speak, and he stills his horse,
                              Sister Helen;
But his words are drowned in the wind's course."
"Nay hear, nay hear, you must hear perforce,
                              Little brother!"
              (O Mother, Mary Mother,
What word now heard, between Hell and Heaven?)   140

"Oh, he says that Keith of Ewern's cry,
                              Sister Helen,
Is ever to see you ere he die."
"In all that his soul sees, there am I,
                              Little brother!"
              (O Mother, Mary Mother,
The soul's one sight, between Hell and Heaven!)

44/Dante Gabriel Rossetti

"He sends a ring and a broken coin,
                    Sister Helen,
And bids you mind the banks of Boyne."   150
"What else he broke will he ever join,
                    Little brother?"
              (O Mother, Mary Mother,
No, never joined, between Hell and Heaven!)

"He yields you these and craves full fain,
                    Sister Helen,
You pardon him in his mortal pain."
"What else he took will he give again,
                    Little brother?"
              (O Mother, Mary Mother,   160
Not twice to give, between Hell and Heaven!)

"He calls your name in an agony,
                    Sister Helen,
That even dead Love must weep to see."
"Hate, born of Love, is blind as he,
                    Little brother!"
              (O Mother, Mary Mother,
Love turned to hate, between Hell and Heaven!)

"Oh it's Keith of Keith now that rides fast,
                    Sister Helen,   170
For I know the white hair on the blast."
"The short, short hour will soon be past,
                    Little brother!"
              (O Mother, Mary Mother,
Will soon be past, between Hell and Heaven!)

"He looks at me and he tries to speak,
                    Sister Helen,
But oh! his voice is sad and weak!"
"What here should the mighty Baron seek,
                    Little brother?"   180
              (O Mother, Mary Mother,
Is this the end, between Hell and Heaven?)

                    Dante Gabriel Rossetti/45

"Oh his son still cries, if you forgive,
                    Sister Helen,
The body dies, but the soul shall live."
"Fire shall forgive me as I forgive,
                    Little brother!"
            (O Mother, Mary Mother,
As she forgives, between Hell and Heaven!)

"Oh he prays you, as his heart would rive,   190
                    Sister Helen,
To save his dear son's soul alive."
"Fire cannot slay it, it shall thrive,
                    Little brother!"
            (O Mother, Mary Mother,
Alas, alas, between Hell and Heaven!)

"He cries to you, kneeling in the road,
                    Sister Helen,
To go with him for the love of God!"
"The way is long to his son's abode,   200
                    Little brother."
            (O Mother, Mary Mother,
The way is long, between Hell and Heaven!)

"A lady's here, by a dark steed brought,
                    Sister Helen,
So darkly clad, I saw her not."
"See her now or never see aught,
                    Little brother!"
            (O Mother, Mary Mother,
What more to see, between Hell and Heaven?)   210

"Her hood falls back, and the moon shines fair
                    Sister Helen,
On the Lady of Ewern's golden hair."
"Blest hour of my power and her despair,
                    Little brother!"
            (O Mother, Mary Mother,
Hour blest and banned, between Hell and Heaven!)

46/Dante Gabriel Rossetti

"Pale, pale her cheeks, that in pride did glow,
     Sister Helen,
'Neath the bridal-wreath three days ago."   220
"One morn for pride and three days for woe,
     Little brother!"
    (O Mother, Mary Mother,
Three days, three nights, between Hell and Heaven!)

"Her clasped hands stretch from her bending head.
     Sister Helen;
With the loud wind's wail her sobs are wed."
"What wedding-strains hath her bridal-bed,
     Little brother?"
    (O Mother, Mary Mother,   230
What strain but death's, between Hell and Heaven?)

"She may not speak, she sinks in a swoon,
     Sister Helen—
She lifts her lips and gasps on the moon."
"Oh! might I but hear her soul's blithe tune,
     Little brother!"
    (O Mother, Mary Mother,
Her woe's dumb cry, between Hell and Heaven!)

"They've caught her to Westholm's saddlebow,
     Sister Helen,   240
And her moonlit hair gleams white in its flow."
"Let it turn whiter than winter snow,
     Little brother!"
    (O Mother, Mary Mother,
Woe-withered gold, between Hell and Heaven!)

"O Sister Helen, you heard the bell,
     Sister Helen!
More loud than the vesper-chime it fell."
"No vesper-chime, but a dying Knell,
     Little brother!"   250
    (O Mother, Mary Mother,
His dying knell, between Hell and Heaven!)

       Dante Gabriel Rossetti/47

"Alas! but I fear the heavy sound,
                    Sister Helen;
Is it in the sky or in the ground?"
"Say, have you turned their horses round,
                    Little brother?"
          (O Mother, Mary Mother,
The lonely ghost, between Hell and Heaven!)

"They have raised the old man from his knee,   260
                    Sister Helen,
And they ride in silence hastily."
"More fast the naked soul doth flee,
                    Little brother!"
          (O Mother, Mary Mother,
The naked soul between Hell and Heaven!)

"Flank to flank are the three steeds gone,
                    Sister Helen,
But the lady's dark steed goes alone."
"And lonely her bridegroom's soul hath flown,   270
                    Little brother."
          (O Mother, Mary Mother,
The lonely ghost between Hell and Heaven!)

"Oh the wind is sad in the iron chill,
                    Sister Helen,
And weary sad they look by the hill."
"But he and I are sadder still,
                    Little brother!"
          (O Mother, Mary Mother,
Most sad of all between Hell and Heaven!)   280

"See, see the wax has dropped from its place,
                    Sister Helen,
And the flames are winning up apace!"
"Yet here they burn but for a space,
                    Little brother!"
          (O Mother, Mary Mother,
Here for a space between Hell and Heaven!)

48/Dante Gabriel Rossetti

"Ah! what white thing at the door has crossed,
                    Sister Helen,
Ah! what is this that sighs in the frost?"   290
"A soul that's lost as mine is lost,
                    Little brother!"
                (O Mother, Mary Mother,
Lost, lost, all lost, between Hell and Heaven!)

MY SISTER'S SLEEP *

She fell asleep on Christmas Eve;
    At length the long-ungranted shade
    Of weary eyelids overweighed
The pain naught else might yet relieve.

Our mother, who had leaned all day
    Over the bed from chime to chime,
    Then raised herself for the first time,
And as she sat her down, did pray.

Her little work-table was spread
    With work to finish. For the glare,   10
    Made by her candle, she had care
To work some distance from the bed.

Without, there was a cold moon up,
    Of winter radiance sheer and thin;
    The hollow halo it was in
Was like an icy crystal cup.

Through the small room, with subtle sound
    Of flame, by vents the fireshine drove
    And reddened. In its dim alcove
The mirror shed a clearness round.   20

* Published in *The Germ*. The subject of the poem is
imaginary and does not refer to Christina Rossetti.

I had been sitting up some nights,
    And my tired mind felt weak and blank;
    Like a sharp strengthening wine it drank
The stillness and the broken lights.

Twelve struck. That sound, by dwindling years
    Heard in each hour, crept off; and then
    The ruffled silence spread again,
Like water that a pebble stirs.

Our mother rose from where she sat;
    Her needles, as she laid them down,   30
    Met lightly, and her silken gown
Settled—no other noise than that.

"Glory unto the Newly Born!"
    So, as said angels, she did say;
    Because we were in Christmas Day,
Though it would still be long till morn.

Just then in the room over us
    There was a pushing back of chairs,
    As some who had sat unawares
So late, now heard the hour, and rose.   40

With anxious, softly-stepping haste
    Our mother went where Margaret lay,
    Fearing the sounds o'erheard—should they
Have broken her long watched-for rest!

She stooped an instant, calm, and turned,
    But suddenly turned back again;
    And all her features seemed in pain
With woe, and her eyes gazed and yearned.

For my part, I but hid my face,
    And held my breath, and spoke no word.   50
    There was none spoken; but I heard
The silence for a little space.

50/*Dante Gabriel Rossetti*

Our mother bowed herself and wept;
   And both my arms fell, and I said,
   "God knows I knew that she was dead."
And there, all white, my sister slept.

Then kneeling, upon Christmas morn
   A little after twelve o'clock
   We said, ere the first quarter struck,
"Christ's blessing on the newly born!"   60

TROY TOWN

Heavenborn Helen, Sparta's queen,
      (O Troy Town!)
Had two breasts of heavenly sheen,
The sun and moon of the heart's desire,
All Love's lordship lay between.
      (O Troy's down,
      Tall Troy's on fire!)

Helen knelt at Venus' shrine,
      (O Troy Town!)
Saying, "A little gift is mine,   10
A little gift for a heart's desire,
Hear me speak and make a sign!
      (O Troy's down,
      Tall Troy's on fire!)

"Look, I bring thee a carven cup;
      (O Troy Town!)
See it here as I hold it up—
Shaped it is to the heart's desire,
Fit to fill when the gods would sup.
      (O Troy's down,   20
      Tall Troy's on fire!)

"It was molded like my breast;

                    (O Troy Town!)
He that sees it may not rest,
Rest at all for his heart's desire.
O give ear to my heart's behest!
        (O Troy's down,
        Tall Troy's on fire!)

"See my breast, how like it is;
        (O Troy Town!)   30
See it bare for the air to kiss!
Is the cup to thy heart's desire?
O for the breast, O make it his!
        (O Troy's down,
        Tall Troy's on fire!)

"Yea, for my bosom here I sue;
        (O Troy Town!)
Thou must give it where 'tis due,
Give it there to the heart's desire.
Whom do I give my bosom to?   40
        (O Troy's down,
        Tall Troy's on fire!)

"Each twin breast is an apple sweet!
        (O Troy Town!)
Once an apple stirred the beat
Of thy heart with the heart's desire—
Say, who brought it then to thy feet?
        (O Troy's down,
        Tall Troy's on fire!)

"They that claimed it then were three;   50
        (O Troy Town!)
For thy sake two hearts did he
Make forlorn of the heart's desire.
Do for him as he did for thee!
        (O Troy's down,
        Tall Troy's on fire!)

52/Dante Gabriel Rossetti

"Mine are apples grown to the south,
   (O Troy Town!)
Grown to taste in the days of drouth,
Taste and waste to the heart's desire;
Mine are apples meet for his mouth!" 60
   (O Troy's down,
   Tall Troy's on fire!)

Venus looked on Helen's gift,
   (O Troy Town!)
Looked and smiled with subtle drift,
Saw the work of her heart's desire—
"There thou kneel'st for Love to lift!"
   (O Troy's down,
   Tall Troy's on fire!) 70

Venus looked in Helen's face,
   (O Troy Town!)
Knew far off an hour and place,
And fire lit from the heart's desire;
Laughed and said, "Thy gift hath grace!"
   (O Troy's down,
   Tall Troy's on fire!)

Cupid looked on Helen's breast,
   (O Troy Town!)
Saw the heart within its nest, 80
Saw the flame of the heart's desire—
Marked his arrow's burning crest.
   (O Troy's down,
   Tall Troy's on fire!)

Cupid took another dart,
   (O Troy Town!)
Fledged it for another heart,
Winged the shaft with the heart's desire,
Drew the string and said, "Depart!"
   (O Troy's down,
   Tall Troy's on fire!) 90

Paris turned upon his bed,
        (O Troy Town!)
Turned upon his bed and said,
Dead at heart with the heart's desire—
"O to clasp her golden head!"
        (O Troy's down,
        Tall Troy's on fire!)

PAX VOBIS *

'Tis of the Father Hilary.
        He strove, but could not pray: so took
        The darkened stair, where his feet shook
A sad blind echo. He kept up
        Slowly. 'Twas a chill sway of air
That autumn noon within the stair,
Sick, dizzy, like a turning cup.
        His brain perplexed him, void and thin:
        He shut his eyes and felt it spin;
        The obscure deafness hemmed him in.   10
He said: "the air is calm outside."

He leaned unto the gallery
        Where the chime keeps the night and day:
        It hurt his brain,—he could not pray.
He had his face upon the stone:
        Deep 'twixt the narrow shafts, his eye
        Passed all the roofs unto the sky
Whose greyness the wind swept alone.
        Close by his feet he saw it shake
        With wind in pools that the rains make: 20
        The ripple set his eyes to ache.
He said, "Calm hath its peace outside."

He stood within the mystery
        Girding God's blessed Eucharist:

* Published in *The Germ*.

The organ and the chaunt had ceased:
A few words paused against his ear,
    Said from the altar: drawn round him,
    The silence was at rest and dim.
He could not pray. The bell shook clear
    And ceased. All was great awe,—the breath   30
    Of God in man, that warranteth
    Wholly the inner things of Faith.
He said: "There is the world outside."

FROM THE CLIFFS: NOON *

The sea is in its listless chime:
    Time's lapse it is, made audible,—
    The murmur of the earth's large shell.
In a sad blueness beyond rhyme
    It ends: sense, without thought, can pass
    No stadium further. Since time was,
This sound hath told the lapse of time.

No stagnance that death wins,—it hath
    The mournfulness of ancient life,
    Always enduring at dull strife.
As the world's heart of rest and wrath,
    Its painful pulse is in the sands.
    Last utterly, the whole sky stands,
Grey and not known, along its path.

SONNETS FROM *The House of Life*

WILLOWWOOD—I

I sat with Love upon a woodside well,
Leaning across the water, I and he;
Nor ever did he speak nor looked at me,
But touched his lute wherein was audible
The certain secret thing he had to tell.

    * Published in *The Germ*.

Dante Gabriel Rossetti/55

Only our mirrored eyes met silently
In the low wave; and that sound came to be
The passionate voice I knew; and my tears fell.
And at their fall, his eyes beneath grew hers;
And with his foot and with his wing-feathers
He swept the spring that watered my heart's drouth.
Then the dark ripples spread to waving hair,
And as I stooped, her own lips rising there
Bubbled with brimming kisses at my mouth.

WILLOWWOOD—2

And now Love sang; but his was such a song,
So meshed with half-remembrance hard to free,
As souls disused in death's sterility
May sing when the new birthday tarries long.
And I was made aware of a dumb throng
That stood aloof, one form by every tree,
All mournful forms, for each was I or she,
The shades of those our days that had no tongue.
They looked on us, and knew us and were known;
While fast together, alive from the abyss,
Clung the soul-wrung implacable close kiss;
And pity of self through all made broken moan
Which said, "For once, for once, for once alone!"
And still Love sang, and what he sang was this:

WILLOWWOOD—3

"O ye, all ye that walk in Willowwood,
That walk with hollow faces burning white:
What fathom-depth of soul-struck widowhood,
What long, what longer hours, one lifelong night,
Ere ye again, who so in vain have wooed
Your last hope lost, who so in vain invite
Your lips to that their unforgotten food,
Ere ye, ere ye again shall see the light!
Alas! the bitter banks in Willowwood,
With tear-spurge wan, with blood-wort burning red.

Alas, if ever such a pillow could
Steep deep the soul in sleep till she were dead—
Better all life forget her than this thing,
That Willowwood should hold her wandering!"

WILLOWWOOD—4

So sang he; and as meeting rose and rose
Together cling through the wind's well-away
Nor change at once, yet near the end of day
The leaves drop loosened where the heart-stain glows—
So when the song died did the kiss unclose;
And her face fell back drowned, and was as gray
As its gray eyes; and if it ever may
Meet mine again I know not if Love knows.
Only I know that I leaned low and drank
A long draft from the water where she sank,
Her breath and all her tears and all her soul;
And as I leaned, I know I felt Love's face
Pressed on my neck with moan of pity and grace,
Till both our heads were in his aureole.

HEART'S HAVEN

Sometimes she is a child within mine arms,
Cowering beneath dark wings that love must
    chase,—
With still tears showering and averted face,
Inexplicably filled with faint alarms:
And oft from mine own spirit's hurtling
    harms
I crave the refuge of her deep embrace,—
Against all ills the fortified strong place
And sweet reserve of sovereign counter-
    charms.
And Love, our light at night and shade at
    noon,
Lulls us to rest with songs, and turns away
All shafts of shelterless tumultuous day.

Dante Gabriel Rossetti/57

Like the moon's growth, his face gleams
    through his tune;
And as soft waters warble to the moon,
Our answering spirits chime one roundelay.

LOVE'S TESTAMENT

O thou who at Love's hour ecstatically
Unto my heart dost evermore present,
Clothed with his fire, thy heart his testament;
Whom I have neared and felt thy breath to be
The inmost incense of his sanctuary;
Who without speech hast owned him, and, intent
Upon his will, thy life with mine hast blent,
And murmured, "I am thine, thou'rt one with me!"
O what from thee the grace, to me the prize,
And what to Love the glory,—when the whole
Of the deep stair thou tread'st to the dim shoal
And weary water of the place of sighs,
And there dost work deliverance, as thine eyes
Draw up my prisoned spirit to thy soul!

VENUS VICTRIX

Could Juno's self more sovereign presence
    wear
Than thou, 'mid other ladies throned in
    grace?—
Or Pallas, when thou bend'st with soul-stilled
    face
O'er poet's page gold-shadowed in thy hair?
Dost thou than Venus seem less heavenly fair
When o'er the sea of love's tumultuous trance
Hovers thy smile, and mingles with thy glance
That sweet voice like the last wave murmuring
    there?
Before such triune loveliness divine
Awestruck I ask, which goddess here most
    claims

The prize that, howso'er adjudged, is thine?
Then Love breathes low the sweetest of thy
    names;
And Venus Victrix to my heart doth bring
Herself, the Helen of thy guerdoning.

GENIUS IN BEAUTY

Beauty like hers is genius. Not the call
Of Homer's or of Dante's heart sublime,—
Not Michael's hand furrowing the zones of
    time,—
Is more with compassed mysteries musical;
Nay, not in Spring's or Summer's sweet
    footfall
More gathered gifts exuberant Life bequeaths
Than doth this sovereign face, whose love-
    spell breathes
Even from its shadowed contour on the wall.
As many men are poets in their youth,
But for one sweet-strung soul the wires pro-
    long
Even through all change the indomitable
    song;
So in likewise the envenomed years, whose
    tooth
Rends shallower grace with ruin void of ruth,
Upon this beauty's power shall wreak no
    wrong.

THE CARILLON *

ANTWERP AND BRUGES

(*In these and others of the Flemish Towns, the Carillon,
or chimes, which have a most fantastic and delicate music,
are played almost continually. The custom is very ancient.*)

At Antwerp, there is a low wall
  Binding the city, and a moat
  Beneath, that the wind keeps afloat.
You pass the gates in a slow drawl
Of wheels. If it is warm at all
  The Carillon will give you thought.

I climbed the stair in Antwerp church,
  What time the urgent weight of sound
  At sunset seems to heave it round.
Far up, the Carillon did search   10
The wind; and the birds came to perch
  Far under, where the gables wound.

In Antwerp harbour on the Scheldt
  I stood along, a certain space
  Of night. The mist was near my face:
Deep on, the flow was heard and felt.
The Carillon kept pause, and dwelt
  In music through the silent place.

At Bruges, when you leave the train,
  —A singing numbness in your ears,—   20
  The Carillon's first sound appears
Only the inner moil. Again
A little minute though—your brain
  Takes quiet, and the whole sense hears.

John Memmeling and John Van Eyck
  Hold state at Bruges. In sore shame
  I scanned the works that keep their name.

  * Published in *The Germ*.

The Carillon, which then did strike
Mine ears, was heard of theirs alike:
   It set me closer unto them.

I climbed at Bruges all the flight
   The belfry has of ancient stone.
   For leagues I saw the east wind blown:
The earth was grey, the sky was white.
   I stood so near upon the height
That my flesh felt the Carillon.

"FOUND"

(For a picture) [1]

"There is a budding morrow in midnight"—
So sang our Keats, our English nightingale.
And here, as lamps across the bridge turn
    pale
In London's smokeless resurrection-light
Dark breaks to dawn. But o'er the deadly
    blight
Of love deflowered and sorrow of none avail
Which makes this man gasp and this woman
    quail,
Can day from darkness ever again take flight?
Ah! gave not these two hearts their mutual pledge,
Under one mantle sheltered 'neath the hedge
In gloaming courtship? And O God! today
He only knows he holds her—but what part
Can life now take? She cries in her locked
    heart,
"Leave me—I do not know you—go away!"

[1] The picture, which Rossetti never finished, shows a young
farmer, who has come to town with a white calf, coming upon
the bedraggled and degraded girl whom he had once loved.

Dante Gabriel Rossetti/61

JOHN KEATS

The weltering London ways where children
    weep
And girls whom none call maidens laugh—
    strange road
Miring his outward steps, who inly trode
The bright Castalian brink and Latmos'
    steep—
Even such his life's cross-paths; till deathly
    deep
He toiled through sands of Lethe; and long
    pain,
Weary with labor spurned and love found
    vain,
In dead Rome's sheltering shadow wrapped
    his sleep.
O pang-dowered Poet, whose reverberant lips
And heart-strung lyre awoke the Moon's
    eclipse—
Thou whom the daisies glory in growing
    o'er—
Their fragrance clings around thy name, not
    writ
But rumored in water, while the fame of it
Along Time's flood goes echoing evermore.

EDEN BOWER

It was Lilith the wife of Adam;
    (*Eden bower's in flower.*)
Not a drop of her blood was human,
But she was made like a soft sweet woman.

Lilith stood on the skirts of Eden;
    (*And O the bower and the hour!*)
She was the first that thence was driven;
With her was hell and with Eve was heaven.

In the ear of the Snake said Lilith:
    (*Eden bower's in flower.*)   10
"To thee I come when the rest is over;
A snake was I when thou wast my lover.

"I was the fairest snake in Eden;
    (*And O the bower and the hour!*)
By the earth's will, new form and feature
Made me a wife for the earth's new creature.

"Take me thou as I come from Adam.
    (*Eden bower's in flower.*)
Once again shall my love subdue thee;
The past is past and I am come to thee.   20

"O but Adam was thrall to Lilith!
    (*And O the bower and the hour!*)
All the threads of my hair are golden,
And there in a net his heart was holden.

"O and Lilith was queen of Adam!
    (*Eden bower's in flower.*)
All the day and the night together
My breath could shake his soul like a feather.

"What great joys had Adam and Lilith!—
    (*And O the bower and the hour!*)   30
Sweet close rings of the serpent's twining,
As heart in heart lay sighing and pining.

"What bright babes had Lilith and Adam!—
    (*Eden bower's in flower.*)
Shapes that coiled in the woods and waters,
Glittering sons and radiant daughters.

"O thou God, the Lord God of Eden!
    (*And O the bower and the hour!*)
Say, was this fair body for no man,
That of Adam's flesh thou mak'st him a
        woman?   40

"O thou Snake, the King-snake of Eden!
    (*Eden bower's in flower.*)
God's strong will our necks are under,
But thou and I may cleave it in sunder.

"Help, sweet Snake, sweet lover of Lilith!
    (*And O the bower and the hour!*)
And let God learn how I loved and hated
Man in the image of God created.

"Help me once against Eve and Adam!
    (*Eden bower's in flower.*)   50
Help me once for this one endeavor,
And then my love shall be thine forever!

"Strong is God, the fell foe of Lilith—
    (*And O the bower and the hour!*)
Naught in heaven or earth may affright him;
But join thou with me and we will smite him.

"Strong is God, the great God of Eden;
    (*Eden bower's in flower.*)
Over all He made He hath power;
But lend me thou thy shape for an hour!   60

"Lend thy shape for the love of Lilith!
    (*And O the bower and the hour!*)
Look, my mouth and my cheek are ruddy,
And thou art cold, and fire is my body.

"Lend thy shape for the hate of Adam!
    (*Eden bower's in flower.*)
That he may wail my joy that forsook him,
And curse the day when the bride-sleep took
   him.

"Lend thy shape for the shame of Eden!
    (*And O the bower and the hour!*)   70
Is not the foe-God weak as the foeman

When love grows hate in the heart of a
  woman?

"Would'st thou know the heart's hope of
  Lilith?
    (*Eden bower's in flower.*)
Then bring thou close thine head till it glisten
Along my breast, and lip me and listen.

"Am I sweet, O sweet Snake of Eden?
    (*And O the bower and the hour!*)
Then ope thine ear to my warm mouth's
  cooing
And learn what deed remains for our doing.   80

"Thou didst hear when God said to Adam:
    (*Eden bower's in flower.*)
'Of all this wealth I have made thee warden;
Thou'rt free to eat of the trees of the garden;

"'Only of one tree eat not in Eden;
    (*And O the bower and the hour!*)
All save one I give to thy freewill—
The Tree of the Knowledge of Good and
  Evil.'

"O my love, come nearer to Lilith!
    (*Eden bower's in flower.*)   90
In thy sweet folds bind me and bend me,
And let me feel the shape thou shalt lend me!

"In thy shape I'll go back to Eden;
    (*And O the bower and the hour!*)
In these coils that Tree will I grapple,
And stretch this crowned head forth by the
  apple.

"Lo, Eve bends to the breath of Lilith!
    (*Eden bower's in flower.*)

Dante Gabriel Rossetti/65

O how then shall my heart desire
All her blood as food to its fire! 100

"Lo, Eve bends to the words of Lilith!—
   (*And O the bower and the hour!*)
'Nay, this Tree's fruit—why should ye
   hate it,
Or death be born the day that ye ate it?

" 'Nay, but on that great day in Eden,
   (*Eden bower's in flower.*)
By the help that in this wise Tree is,
God knows well ye shall be as He is.'

"Then Eve shall eat and give unto Adam;
   (*And O the bower and the hour!*) 110
And then they both shall know they are
   naked,
And their hearts ache as my heart hath achéd.

"Aye, let them hide in the trees of Eden,
   (*Eden bower's in flower.*)
As in the cool of the day in the garden
God shall walk without pity or pardon.

"Hear, thou Eve, the man's heart in Adam!
   (*And O the bower and the hour!*)
Of his brave words hark to the bravest:
'This the woman gave that thou gavest.' 120

"Hear Eve speak, yea, list to her, Lilith!
   (*Eden bower's in flower.*)
Feast thine heart with words that shall sate
   it—
'This the serpent gave and I ate it.'

"O proud Eve, cling close to thine Adam,
   (*And O the bower and the hour!*)
Driven forth as the beasts of his naming
By the sword that forever is flaming.

66/*Dante Gabriel Rossetti*

"Know, thy path is known unto Lilith!
    (*Eden bower's in flower.*)   130
While the blithe birds sang at thy wedding.
There her tears grew thorns for thy threading.

"O my love, thou Love-snake of Eden!
    (*And O the bower and the hour!*)
O today and the day to come after!
Loose me, love—give breath to my laughter!

"O bright Snake, the Death-worm of Adam!
    (*Eden bower's in flower.*)
Wreathe thy neck with my hair's bright
  tether,
And wear my gold and thy gold together!   140

"On that day on the skirts of Eden,
    (*And O the bower and the hour!*)
In thy shape shall I glide back to thee,
And in my shape for an instant view thee.

"But when thou'rt thou and Lilith is Lilith,
    (*Eden bower's in flower.*)
In what bliss past hearing or seeing
Shall each one drink of the other's being!

"With cries of 'Eve!' and 'Eden!' and 'Adam!'
    (*And O the bower and the hour!*)   150
How shall we mingle our love's caresses,
I in thy coils, and thou in my tresses!

"With those names, ye echoes of Eden,
    (*Eden bower's in flower.*)
Fire shall cry from my heart that burneth—
'Dust he is and to dust returneth!'

"Yet today, thou master of Lilith—
    (*And O the bower and the hour!*)
Wrap me round in the form I'll borrow
And let me tell thee of sweet tomorrow.   160

"In the planted garden eastward in Eden,
  (*Eden bower's in flower.*)
Where the river goes forth to water the garden,
The springs shall dry and the soil shall harden.

"Yea, where the bride-sleep fell upon Adam,
  (*And O the bower and the hour!*)
None shall hear when the storm-wind whistles
Through roses choked among thorns and thistles.

"Yea, beside the east-gate of Eden,
  (*Eden bower's in flower.*)   170
Where God joined them and none might sever
The sword turns this way and that forever.

"What of Adam cast out of Eden?
  (*And O the bower and the hour!*)
Lo! with care like a shadow shaken,
He tills the hard earth whence he was taken.

"What of Eve too, cast out of Eden?
  (*Eden bower's in flower.*)
Nay, but she, the bride of God's giving,
Must yet be mother of all men living.   180

"Lo, God's grace, by the grace of Lilith!
  (*And O the bower and the hour!*)
To Eve's womb, from our sweet tomorrow,
God shall greatly multiply sorrow.

"Fold me fast, O God-snake of Eden!
  (*Eden bower's in flower.*)
What more prize than love to impel thee?
Grip and lip my limbs as I tell thee!

"Lo! two babes for Eve and for Adam!
  (*And O the bower and the hour!*)   190

Lo! sweet Snake, the travail and treasure—
Two men-children born for their pleasure!

"The first is Cain and the second Abel;
    (*Eden bower's in flower.*)
The soul of one shall be made thy brother,
And thy tongue shall lap the blood of the
    other."
    (*And O the bower and the hour!*)

THE BALLAD OF DEAD LADIES

(FROM FRANÇOIS VILLON) [1]

Tell me now in what hidden way is
    Lady Flora the lovely Roman?
Where's Hipparchia, and where is Thais,
    Neither of them the fairer woman?
    Where is Echo, beheld of no man,
Only heard on river and mere—
    She whose beauty was more than hu-
      man? . . .
But where are the snows of yester-year?

Where's Héloise, the learned nun,
    For whose sake Abeillard, I ween,   10
Lost manhood and put priesthood on?
    (From Love he won such dule and teen!)
    And where, I pray you, is the Queen
Who willed that Buridan should steer
    Sewed in a sack's mouth down the Seine? . . .
But where are the snows of yester-year?

White Queen Blanche, like a queen of lilies,
    With a voice like any mermaiden—
Bertha Broadfoot, Beatrice, Alice,

[1] Translated from François Villon's *Ballade des Dames du Temps Jadis*.

And Ermengarde the lady of Maine—
And that good Joan whom Englishmen
At Rouen doomed and burned her there—
Mother of God, where are they then? . . .
But where are the snows of yester-year?

Nay, never ask this week, fair lord,
Where they are gone, nor yet this year,
Except with this for an overword—
But where are the snows of yester-year?

GOBLIN MARKET

Morning and evening
Maids heard the goblins cry,
"Come buy our orchard fruits,
Come buy, come buy:
Apples and quinces,
Lemons and oranges,
Plump unpecked cherries,
Melons and raspberries,
Bloom-down-cheeked peaches,
Swart-headed mulberries,   10
Wild free-born cranberries,
Crab-apples, dewberries,
Pineapples, blackberries,
Apricots, strawberries—
All ripe together
In summer weather—
Morns that pass by,
Fair eves that fly;
Come buy, come buy:
Our grapes fresh from the vine,   20
Pomegranates full and fine,
Dates and sharp bullaces,
Rare pears and greengages,
Damsons and bilberries,
Taste them and try;
Currants and gooseberries,
Bright-fire-like barberries,
Figs to fill your mouth,
Citrons from the South,
Sweet to tongue and sound to eye;   30
Come buy, come buy."

Evening by evening
Among the brook-side rushes,

Laura bowed her head to hear,
Lizzie veiled her blushes;
Crouching close together
In the cooling weather,
With clasping arms and cautioning lips,
With tingling cheeks and finger tips.
"Lie close," Laura said,   40
Pricking up her golden head.
"We must not look at goblin men,
We must not buy their fruits;
Who knows upon what soil they fed
Their hungry thirsty roots?"
"Come buy," call the goblins
Hobbling down the glen.
"Oh," cried Lizzie, "Laura, Laura,
You should not peep at goblin men."
Lizzie covered up her eyes,   50
Covered close lest they should look;
Laura reared her glossy head,
And whispered like the restless brook:
"Look, Lizzie, look, Lizzie,
Down the glen tramp little men.
One hauls a basket,
One bears a plate,
One lugs a golden dish
Of many pounds' weight.
How fair the vine must grow   60
Whose grapes are so luscious!
How warm the wind must blow
Through those fruit bushes!"
"No," said Lizzie, "No, no, no;
Their offers should not charm us,
Their evil gifts would harm us."
She thrust a dimpled finger
In each ear, shut eyes and ran.
Curious Laura chose to linger,
Wondering at each merchant man.   70
One had a cat's face,
One whisked a tail,

72/*Christina Rossetti*

One tramped at a rat's pace,
One crawled like a snail,
One like a wombat prowled obtuse and furry,
One like a ratel tumbled hurry-skurry.
She heard a voice like voice of doves
Cooing all together;
They sounded kind and full of loves
In the pleasant weather.   80

Laura stretched her gleaming neck
Like a rush-imbedded swan,
Like a lily from the beck,
Like a moonlit poplar branch,
Like a vessel at the launch
When its last restraint is gone.

Backward up the mossy glen
Turned and trooped the goblin men,
With their shrill repeated cry,
"Come buy, come buy."   90
When they reached where Laura was
They stood stock still upon the moss,
Leering at each other,
Brother with queer brother;
Signaling each other,
Brother with sly brother.
One set his basket down,
One reared his plate;
One began to weave a crown
Of tendrils, leaves, and rough nuts brown   100
(Men sell not such in any town);
One heaved the golden weight
Of dish and fruit to offer her:
"Come buy, come buy" was still their cry.
Laura stared but did not stir,
Longed but had no money.
The whisk-tailed merchant bade her taste
In tones as smooth as honey,
The cat-faced purred,

The rat-paced spoke a word
Of welcome, and the snail-paced even was heard;
One parrot-voiced and jolly
Cried, "Pretty Goblin" still for "Pretty Polly";
One whistled like a bird.

But sweet-tooth Laura spoke in haste:
"Good folk, I have no coin;
To take were to purloin.
I have no copper in my purse,
I have no silver either,
And all my gold is on the furze   120
That shakes in windy weather
Above the rusty heather."
"You have much gold upon your head,"
They answered all together;
"Buy from us with a golden curl."
She clipped a precious golden lock,
She dropped a tear more rare than pearl,
Then sucked their fruit globes fair or red.
Sweeter than honey from the rock,
Stronger than man-rejoicing wine,   130
Clearer than water flowed that juice;
She never tasted such before,
How should it cloy with length of use?
She sucked and sucked and sucked the more
Fruits which that unknown orchard bore;
She sucked until her lips were sore;
Then flung the emptied rinds away,
But gathered up one kernel stone,
And knew not was it night or day
As she turned home alone.   140

Lizzie met her at the gate,
Full of wise upbraidings:
"Dear, you should not stay so late,
Twilight is not good for maidens;
Should not loiter in the glen
In the haunts of goblin men.

Do you not remember Jeanie,
How she met them in the moonlight,
Took their gifts both choice and many,
Ate their fruits and wore their flowers   150
Plucked from bowers
Where summer ripens at all hours?
But ever in the moonlight
She pined and pined away;
Sought them by night and day,
Found them no more, but dwindled and grew gray;
Then fell with the first snow,
While to this day no grass will grow
Where she lies low;
I planted daisies there a year ago   160
That never blow.
You should not loiter so."
"Nay, hush," said Laura;
"Nay, hush, my sister.
I ate and ate my fill,
Yet my mouth waters still.
Tomorrow night I will
Buy more"; and kissed her.
"Have done with sorrow;
I'll bring you plums tomorrow   170
Fresh on their mother twigs,
Cherries worth getting;
You cannot think what figs
My teeth have met in,
What melons icy-cold
Piled on a dish of gold
Too huge for me to hold,
What peaches with a velvet nap,
Pellucid grapes without one seed.
Odorous indeed must be the mead   180
Whereon they grow, and pure the wave they drink
With lilies at the brink,
And sugar-sweet their sap."

Golden head by golden head,

Like two pigeons in one nest
Folded in each other's wings,
They lay down in their curtained bed;
Like two blossoms on one stem,
Like two flakes of new-fall'n snow,
Like two wands of ivory   190
Tipped with gold for awful kings.
Moon and stars gazed in at them,
Wind sang to them lullaby,
Lumbering owls forebore to fly,
Not a bat flapped to and fro
Round their nest;
Cheek to cheek and breast to breast
Locked together in one nest.

Early in the morning
When the first cock crowed his warning,   200
Neat like bees, as sweet and busy,
Laura rose with Lizzie;
Fetched in honey, milked the cows,
Aired and set to rights the house,
Kneaded cakes of whitest wheat,
Cakes for dainty mouths to eat,
Next churned butter, whipped up cream,
Fed their poultry, sat and sewed;
Talked as modest maidens should—
Lizzie with an open heart,   210
Laura in an absent dream,
One content, one sick in part;
One warbling for the mere bright day's delight,
One longing for the night.

At length slow evening came.
They went with pitchers to the reedy brook;
Lizzie most placid in her look,
Laura most like a leaping flame.
They drew the gurgling water from its deep.
Lizzie plucked purple and rich golden flags,   220
Then turning homeward said: "The sunset flushes

Those furthest loftiest crags;
Come, Laura, not another maiden lags.
No willful squirrel wags;
The beasts and birds are fast asleep."

But Laura loitered still among the rushes,
And said the bank was steep,
And said the hour was early still,
The dew not fall'n, the wind not chill;
Listening ever, but not catching   230
The customary cry,
"Come buy, come buy,"
With its iterated jingle
Of sugar-baited words;
Not for all her watching
Once discerning even one goblin
Racing, whisking, tumbling, hobbling—
Let alone the herds
That used to tramp along the glen,
In groups or single,   240
Of brisk fruit-merchant men.

Till Lizzie urged, "O Laura, come;
I hear the fruit-call, but I dare not look.
You should not loiter longer at this brook;
Come with me home.
The stars rise, the moon bends her arc,
Each glowworm winks her spark,
Let us get home before the night grows dark,
For clouds may gather
Though this is summer weather,   250
Put out the lights and drench us through;
Then if we lost our way what should we do?"

Laura turned cold as stone
To find her sister heard that cry alone,
That goblin cry,
"Come buy our fruits, come buy."
Must she then buy no more such dainty fruit?

Must she no more such succous pasture find,
Gone deaf and blind?
Her tree of life drooped from the root;   260
She said not one word in her heart's sore ache;
But peering through the dimness, naught discerning,
Trudged home, her pitcher dripping all the way;
So crept to bed, and lay
Silent till Lizzie slept;
Then sat up in a passionate yearning,
And gnashed her teeth for balked desire, and wept
As if her heart would break.

Day after day, night after night,
Laura kept watch in vain   270
In sullen silence of exceeding pain.
She never caught again the goblin cry,
"Come buy, come buy";
She never spied the goblin men
Hawking their fruits along the glen.
But when the noon waxed bright
Her hair grew thin and gray;
She dwindled, as the fair full moon doth turn
To swift decay and burn
Her fire away.   280

One day, remembering her kernel-stone,
She set it by a wall that faced the south;
Dewed it with tears, hoped for a root,
Watched for a waxing shoot,
But there came none.
It never saw the sun,
It never felt the trickling moisture run;
While with sunk eyes and faded mouth
She dreamed of melons, as a traveler sees
False waves in desert drouth   290
With shade of leaf-crowned trees,
And burns the thirstier in the sandful breeze.

She no more swept the house,

Tended the fowls or cows,
Fetched honey, kneaded cakes of wheat,
Brought water from the brook;
But sat down listless in the chimney-nook
And would not eat.

Tender Lizzie could not bear
To watch her sister's cankerous care,   300
Yet not to share.
She night and morning
Caught the goblins' cry:
"Come buy our orchard fruits,
Come buy, come buy."
Beside the brook, along the glen,
She heard the tramp of goblin men,
The voice and stir
Poor Laura could not hear;
Longed to buy fruit to comfort her,   310
But feared to pay too dear.
She thought of Jeanie in her grave,
Who should have been a bride;
But who for joys brides hope to have
Fell sick and died
In her gay prime,
In earliest winter time,
With the first glazing rime,
With the first snow-fall of crisp winter time.

Till Laura dwindling   320
Seemed knocking at Death's door.
Then Lizzie weighed no more
Better and worse;
But put a silver penny in her purse,
Kissed Laura, crossed the heath with clumps of furze
At twilight, halted by the brook,
And for the first time in her life
Began to listen and look.

Laughed every goblin

When they spied her peeping;
Came toward her hobbling,
Flying, running, leaping,
Puffing and blowing,
Chuckling, clapping, crowing,
Clucking and gobbling,
Mopping and mowing,
Full of airs and graces,
Pulling wry faces
Demure grimaces,
Cat-like and rat-like, 340
Ratel- and wombat-like,
Snail-paced in a hurry,
Parrot-voiced and whistler,
Helter-skelter, hurry-skurry,
Chattering like magpies,
Fluttering like pigeons,
Gliding like fishes—
Hugged her and kissed her,
Squeezed and caressed her,
Stretched up their dishes, 350
Panniers, and plates:
"Look at our apples
Russet and dun,
Bob at our cherries,
Bite at our peaches,
Citrons and dates,
Grapes for the asking,
Pears red with basking
Out in the sun,
Plums on their twigs; 360
Pluck them and suck them—
Pomegranates, figs."

"Good folk," said Lizzie,
Mindful of Jeanie,
"Give me much and many";
Held out her apron,
Tossed them her penny.

"Nay, take a seat with us,
Honor and eat with us,"
They answered, grinning; 370
"Our feast is but beginning.
Night yet is early,
Warm and dew-pearly,
Wakeful and starry.
Such fruits as these
No man can carry;
Half their bloom would fly,
Half their dew would dry,
Half their flavor would pass by.
Sit down and feast with us, 380
Be welcome guest with us,
Cheer you and rest with us."—
"Thank you," said Lizzie, "but one waits
At home alone for me;
So without further parleying,
If you will not sell me any
Of your fruits though much and many,
Give me back my silver penny
I tossed you for a fee."—
They began to scratch their pates, 390
No longer wagging, purring,
But visibly demurring,
Grunting and snarling.
One called her proud,
Cross-grained, uncivil;
Their tones waxed loud,
Their looks were evil.
Lashing their tails,
They trod and hustled her,
Elbowed and jostled her, 400
Clawed with their nails,
Barking, mewing, hissing, mocking,
Tore her gown and soiled her stocking,
Twitched her hair out by the roots,
Stamped upon her tender feet,
Held her hands and squeezed their fruits

Against her mouth to make her eat.

White and golden Lizzie stood,
Like a lily in a flood—
Like a rock of blue-veined stone   410
Lashed by tides obstreperously—
Like a beacon left alone
In a hoary, roaring sea,
Sending up a golden fire—
Like a fruit-crowned orange-tree
White with blossoms honey-sweet
Sore beset by wasp and bee—
Like a royal virgin town
Topped with gilded dome and spire
Close beleaguered by a fleet   420
Mad to tug her standard down.

One may lead a horse to water;
Twenty cannot make him drink.
Though the goblins cuffed and caught her,
Coaxed and fought her,
Bullied and besought her,
Scratched her, pinched her black as ink,
Kicked and knocked her,
Mauled and mocked her,
Lizzie uttered not a word;   430
Would not open lip from lip
Lest they should cram a mouthful in;
But laughed in heart to feel the drip
Of juice that siruped all her face,
And lodged in dimples of her chin,
And streaked her neck which quaked like curd.
At last the evil people,
Worn out by her resistance,
Flung back her penny, kicked their fruit
Along whichever road they took,   440
Not leaving root or stone or shoot;
Some writhed into the ground,
Some dived into the brook

With ring and ripple,
Some scudded on the gale without a sound,
Some vanished in the distance.

In a smart, ache, tingle,
Lizzie went her way;
Knew not was it night or day;
Sprang up the bank, tore through the furze,   450
Threaded copse and dingle,
And heard her penny jingle
Bouncing in her purse—
Its bounce was music to her ear.
She ran and ran
As if she feared some goblin man
Dogged her with gibe or curse
Or something worse;
But not one goblin skurried after,
Nor was she pricked by fear;   460
The kind heart made her windy-paced
That urged her home quite out of breath with haste
And inward laughter.

She cried, "Laura," up the garden,
"Did you miss me?
Come and kiss me.
Never mind my bruises,
Hug me, kiss me, suck my juices
Squeezed from goblin fruits for you,
Goblin pulp and goblin dew.   470
Eat me, drink me, love me;
Laura, make much of me;
For your sake I have braved the glen
And had to do with goblin merchant men."

Laura started from her chair,
Flung her arms up in the air,
Clutched her hair:
"Lizzie, Lizzie, have you tasted
For my sake the fruit forbidden,

Must your light like mine be hidden, 480
Your young life like mine be wasted,
Undone in mine undoing,
And ruined in my ruin,
Thirsty, cankered, goblin-ridden?"—
She clung about her sister,
Kissed and kissed and kissed her;
Tears once again
Refreshed her shrunken eyes,
Dropping like rain
After long sultry drouth; 490
Shaking with aguish fear, and pain,
She kissed and kissed her with a hungry mouth.
Her lips began to scorch,
That juice was wormwood to her tongue,
She loathed the feast.
Writhing as one possessed, she leaped and sung,
Rent all her robe, and wrung
Her hands in lamentable haste,
And beat her breast.
Her locks streamed like the torch 500
Borne by a racer at full speed,
Or like the mane of horses in their flight,
Or like an eagle when she stems the light
Straight toward the sun,
Or like a caged thing freed,
Or like a flying flag when armies run.

Swift fire spread through her veins, knocked at her heart,
Met the fire smoldering there
And overbore its lesser flame;
She gorged on bitterness without a name— 510
Ah, fool, to choose such part
Of soul-consuming care!
Sense failed in the mortal strife;
Like the watch-tower of a town
Which an earthquake shatters down,
Like a lightning-stricken mast,
Like a wind-uprooted tree

Spun about,
Like a foam-topped waterspout
Cast down headlong in the sea,   520
She fell at last;
Pleasure past and anguish past,
Is it death or is it life?

Life out of death.
That night long Lizzie watched by her,
Counted her pulse's flagging stir,
Felt for her breath,
Held water to her lips, and cooled her face
With tears and fanning leaves.
But when the first birds chirped about their eaves,   530
And early reapers plodded to the place
Of golden sheaves,
And dew-wet grass
Bowed in the morning winds so brisk to pass,
And new buds with new day
Opened of cup-like lilies on the stream,
Laura awoke as from a dream,
Laughed in the innocent old way,
Hugged Lizzie but not twice or thrice;
Her gleaming locks showed not one thread of gray,   540
Her breath was sweet as May,
And light danced in her eyes.

Days, weeks, months, years
Afterwards, when both were wives
With children of their own;
Their mother-hearts beset with fears,
Their lives bound up in tender lives;
Laura would call the little ones
And tell them of her early prime,
Those pleasant days long gone   550
Of not-returning time;
Would talk about the haunted glen,
The wicked quaint fruit-merchant men,
Their fruits like honey to the throat

But poison in the blood
(Men sell not such in any town);
Would tell them how her sister stood
In deadly peril to do her good,
And win the fiery antidote;
Then joining hands to little hands   560
Would bid them cling together—
"For there is no friend like a sister
In calm or stormy weather;
To cheer one on the tedious way,
To fetch one if one goes astray,
To lift one if one totters down,
To strengthen whilst one stands."

SONG

When I am dead, my dearest,
   Sing no sad songs for me;
Plant thou no roses at my head,
   Nor shady cypress tree.
Be the green grass above me
   With showers and dewdrops wet;
And if thou wilt, remember,
   And if thou wilt, forget.

I shall not see the shadows,
   I shall not feel the rain;
I shall not hear the nightingale
   Sing on as if in pain.
And dreaming through the twilight
   That doth not rise nor set,
Haply I may remember,
   And haply may forget.

DREAM LAND*

Where sunless rivers weep
Their waves into the deep,
She sleeps a charmèd sleep;
   Awake her not.
Led by a single star,
She came from very far
To seek where shadows are
   Her pleasant lot.

She left the rosy morn,
She left the fields of corn,   **10**
For twilight cold and lorn
   And water springs.
Through sleep, as through a veil,
She sees the sky look pale,
And hears the nightingale
   That sadly sings.

Rest, rest, a perfect rest
Shed over brow and breast;
Her face is toward the west,
   The purple land.   **20**
She cannot see the grain
Ripening on hill and plain,
She cannot feel the rain
   Upon her hand.

Rest, rest, for evermore
Upon a mossy shore;
Rest, rest at the heart's core
   Till time shall cease:
Sleep that no pain shall wake;
Night that no morn shall break,   **30**
Till joy shall overtake
   Her perfect peace.

* Published in *The Germ.*

Christina Rossetti/87

THE THREE ENEMIES

THE FLESH

"Sweet, thou art pale."
                      "More pale to see,
Christ hung upon the cruel tree
And bore His Father's wrath for me."

"Sweet, thou art sad."
                    "Beneath a rod
More heavy, Christ for my sake trod
The winepress of the wrath of God."

"Sweet, thou art weary."
                    "Not so Christ,
Whose mighty love of me sufficed
For Strength, Salvation, Eucharist."

"Sweet, thou art footsore."
                    "If I bleed,   **10**
His feet have bled; yea, in my need
His Heart once bled for mine indeed."

THE WORLD

"Sweet, thou art young."
                    "So He was young
Who for my sake in silence hung
Upon the Cross with Passion wrung."

"Look, thou art fair."
                    "He was more fair
Than men, Who deigned for me to wear
A visage marred beyond compare."

"And thou hast riches."
                    "Daily bread;
All else is His—Who, living, dead,   **20**

For me lacked where to lay His Head."

"And life is sweet."

                           "It was not so
To Him, Whose Cup did overflow
With mine unutterable woe."

THE DEVIL

"Thou drinkest deep."

                          "When Christ would sup
He drained the dregs from out my cup;
So how should I be lifted up?"

"Thou shalt win Glory."

                          "In the skies,
Lord Jesus, cover up mine eyes
Lest they should look on vanities."   30

"Thou shalt have Knowledge."

                          "Helpless dust!
In Thee, O Lord, I put my trust;
Answer Thou for me, Wise and Just."

"And Might."—

                          "Get thee behind me. Lord,
Who hast redeemed and not abhorred
My soul, oh, keep it by Thy Word."

AT HOME

When I was dead, my spirit turned
   To seek the much-frequented house.
I passed the door, and saw my friends
   Feasting beneath green orange-boughs;
From hand to hand they pushed the wine,
   They sucked the pulp of plum and peach;

Christina Rossetti/89

They sang, they jested, and they laughed,
    For each was loved of each.

I listened to their honest chat.
    Said one: "Tomorrow we shall be   10
Plod plod along the featureless sands,
    And coasting miles and miles of sea."
Said one: "Before the turn of tide
    We will achieve the eyrie-seat."
Said one: "Tomorrow shall be like
    Today, but much more sweet."

"Tomorrow," said they, strong with hope,
    And dwelt upon the pleasant way.
"Tomorrow," cried they one and all,
    While no one spoke of yesterday.   20
Their life stood full at blessed noon;
    I, only I, had passed away.
"Tomorrow and today," they cried;
    I was of yesterday.

I shivered comfortless, but cast
    No chill across the tablecloth;
I, all-forgotten, shivered, sad
    To stay and yet to part how loath;
I passed from the familiar room,
    I who from love had passed away,   30
Like the remembrance of a guest
    That tarrieth but a day.

AMOR MUNDI

"Oh, where are you going with your lovelocks flowing,
    On the west wind blowing along this valley track?"
"The downhill path is easy, come with me an it please ye,
    We shall escape the uphill by never turning back."

So they two went together in glowing August weather,
  The honey-breathing heather lay to their left and right;
And dear she was to doat on, her swift feet seemed to float on
  The air like soft twin pigeons too sportive to alight.

"Oh, what is that in heaven where gray cloud-flakes are seven,
  Where blackest clouds hang riven just at the rainy
    skirt?"   10
"Oh, that's a meteor sent us, a message dumb, portentous,
  An undeciphered solemn signal of help or hurt."

"Oh, what is that glides quickly where velvet flowers grow
    thickly,
  Their scent comes rich and sickly?" "A scaled and hooded
    worm."
"Oh, what's that in the hollow, so pale I quake to follow?"
  "Oh, that's a thin dead body which waits the eternal term."

"Turn again, O my sweetest—turn again, false and fleetest;
  This beaten way thou beatest, I fear, is hell's own track."
"Nay, too steep for hill mounting; nay, too late for cost
    counting;
  This downhill path is easy, but there's no turning back." 20

AN END*

Love, strong as death, is dead.
  Come let us make his bed
    Among the dying flowers:
A green turf at his head;
And a stone at his feet,
  Whereon we may sit
    In the quiet evening hours.

He was born in the spring,

  * Published in *The Germ*.

And died before the harvesting.
    On the last warm summer day   10
    He left us;—he would not stay
    For autumn twilight cold and grey.
Sit we by his grave and sing
    He is gone away.
To few chords, and sad, and low,
    Sing we so.
Be our eyes fixed on the grass,
  Shadow-veiled, as the years pass,
While we think of all that was
    In the long ago.   20

A TESTIMONY*

I said of laughter: It is vain;—
    Of mirth I said: What profits it?—
    Therefore I found a book, and writ
Therein, how ease and also pain,
How health and sickness, every one
Is vanity beneath the sun.

Man walks in a vain shadow; he
    Disquieteth himself in vain.
    The things that were shall be again.
The rivers do not fill the sea,   10
But turn back to their secret source:
The winds, too, turn upon their course.

Our treasures, moth and rust corrupt;
    Or thieves break through and steal; or they
    Make themselves wings and fly away.
One man made merry as he supp'd,
Nor guessed how when that night grew dim,
His soul would be required of him.

    * Published in *The Germ*.

We build our houses on the sand
    Comely withoutside, and within;   20
    But when the winds and rains begin
To beat on them, they cannot stand;
They perish, quickly overthrown,
Loose at the hidden basement stone.

All things are vanity, I said:
    Yea vanity of vanities.
    The rich man dies; and the poor dies:
The worm feeds sweetly on the dead.
Whatso thou lackest, keep this trust:—
All in the end shall have but dust.   30

The one inheritance, which best
    And worst alike shall find and share.
    The wicked cease from troubling there,
And there the weary are at rest;
There all the wisdom of the wise
Is vanity of vanities.

Man flourishes as a green leaf,
    And as a leaf doth pass away;
    Or, as a shade that cannot stay,
And leaves no track, his course is brief: 40
Yet doth man hope and fear and plan
Till he is dead:—oh foolish man!

Our eyes cannot be satisfied
    With seeing; nor our ears be fill'd
    With hearing: yet we plant and build,
And buy, and make our borders wide:
We gather wealth, we gather care,
But know not who shall be our heir.

Why should we hasten to arise
    So early, and so late take rest?   50
    Our labor is not good; our best
Hopes fade; our heart is stayed on lies:

Verily, we sow wind; and we
Shall reap the whirlwind, verily.

He who hath little shall not lack;
  He who hath plenty shall decay:
  Our fathers went; we pass away;
Our children follow on our track:
So generations fail, and so
They are renewed, and come and go.   60

The earth is fattened with our dead;
  She swallows more and doth not cease:
  Therefore her wine and oil increase
And her sheaves are not numbered;
Therefore her plants are green, and all
Her pleasant trees lusty and tall.

Therefore the maidens cease to sing,
  And the young men are very sad;
  Therefore the sowing is not glad,
And weary is the harvesting.   70
Of high and low, of great and small,
Vanity is the lot of all.

A king dwelt in Jerusalem:
  He was the wisest man on earth;
  He had all riches from his birth,
And pleasures till he tired of them:
Then, having tested all things, he
Witnessed that all are vanity.

REPINING*

She sat alway thro' the long day
  Spinning the weary thread away;
  And ever said in undertone:
"Come, that I be no more alone."

  * Published in *The Germ*.

94/*Christina Rossetti*

From early dawn to set of sun
Working, her task was still undone;
And the long thread seemed to increase
Even while she spun and did not cease.
She heard the gentle turtle-dove
Tell to its mate a tale of love;
She saw the glancing swallows fly,
Ever a social company;
She knew each bird upon its nest
Had cheering songs to bring it rest;
None lived alone save only she;—
The wheel went round more wearily;
She wept and said in undertone:
"Come, that I be no more alone."

Day followed day, and still she sighed
For love, and was not satisfied;
Until one night, when the moonlight
Turned all the trees to silver white,
She heard, what ne'er she heard before,
A steady hand undo the door.
The nightingale since set of sun
Her throbbing music had not done,
And she had listened silently;
But now the wind had changed, and she
Heard the sweet song no more, but heard
Beside her bed a whispered word:
"Damsel, rise up; be not afraid;
For I am come at last," it said.

She trembled, tho' the voice was mild;
She trembled like a frightened child;—
Till she looked up, and then she saw
The unknown speaker without awe.
He seemed a fair young man, his eyes
Beaming with serious charities;
His cheek was white, but hardly pale;
And a dim glory like a veil
Hovered about his head, and shone
Thro' the whole room till night was gone.

10

20

30

40

Christina Rossetti/95

So her fear fled; and then she said,
Leaning upon her quiet bed:
"Now thou art come, I prithee stay,
That I may see thee in the day,
And learn to know thy voice, and hear
It evermore calling me near."

He answered: "Rise, and follow me."
But she looked upwards wonderingly: 50
"And whither would'st thou go, friend? stay
Until the dawning of the day."
But he said: "The wind ceaseth, Maid;
Of chill nor damp be thou afraid."

She bound her hair up from the floor,
And passed in silence from the door.

So they went forth together, he
Helping her forward tenderly.
The hedges bowed beneath his hand;
Forth from the streams came the dry land   60
As they passed over; evermore
The pallid moonbeams shone before;
And the wind hushed, and nothing stirred;
Not even a solitary bird,
Scared by their footsteps, fluttered by
Where aspen-trees stood steadily.

As they went on, at length a sound
Came trembling on the air around;
The undistinguishable hum
Of life, voices that go and come   70
Of busy men, and the child's sweet
High laugh, and noise of trampling feet.

Then he said: "Wilt thou go and see?"
And she made answer joyfully;
"The noise of life, of human life,
Of dear communion without strife,

Of converse held 'twixt friend and friend;
Is it not here our path shall end?"
He led her on a little way
Until they reached a hillock: "Stay."   80
It was a village in a plain.
High mountains screened it from the rain
And stormy wind; and nigh at hand
A bubbling streamlet flowed, o'er sand
Pebbly and fine, and sent life up
Green succous stalk and flower-cup.

Gradually, day's harbinger,
A chilly wind began to stir.
It seemed a gentle powerless breeze
That scarcely rustled thro' the trees;   90
And yet it touched the mountain's head
And the paths man might never tread.
But hearken: in the quiet weather
Do all the streams flow down together?—
No, 'tis a sound more terrible
Than tho' a thousand rivers fell.
The everlasting ice and snow
Were loosened then, but not to flow;—
With a loud crash like solid thunder
The avalanche came, burying under   100
The village; turning life and breath
And rest and joy and plans to death.

"Oh! let us fly, for pity fly;
Let us go hence, friend, thou and I.
There must be many regions yet
Where these things make not desolate."
He looked upon her seriously;
Then said: "Arise and follow me."
The path that lay before them was
Nigh covered over with long grass;   110
And many slimy things and slow
Trailed on between the roots below.
The moon looked dimmer than before;

And shadowy cloudlets floating o'er
Its face sometimes quite hid its light,
And filled the skies with deeper night.

At last, as they went on, the noise
Was heard of the sea's mighty voice;
And soon the ocean could be seen
In its long restlessness serene.   120
Upon its breast a vessel rode
That drowsily appeared to nod
As the great billows rose and fell,
And swelled to sink, and sank to swell.

Meanwhile the strong wind had come forth
From the chill regions of the North,
The mighty wind invisible.
And the low waves began to swell;
And the sky darkened overhead;
And the moon once looked forth, then fled   130
Behind dark clouds; while here and there
The lightning shone out in the air;
And the approaching thunder rolled
With angry pealings manifold.
How many vows were made, and prayers
That in safe times were cold and scarce.
Still all availed not; and at length
The waves arose in all their strength,
And fought against the ship, and filled
The ship. Then were the clouds unsealed,   140
And the rain hurried forth, and beat
On every side and over it.

Some clung together, and some kept
A long stern silence, and some wept.
Many half-crazed looked on in wonder
As the strong timbers rent asunder;
Friends forgot friends, foes fled to foes;—
And still the water rose and rose.

"Ah woe is me! Whom I have seen
Are now as tho' they had not been.   150
In the earth there is room for birth,
And there are graves enough in earth;
Why should the cold sea, tempest-torn,
Bury those whom it hath not borne?"

He answered not, and they went on.
The glory of the heavens was gone;
The moon gleamed not nor any star;
Cold winds were rustling near and far,
And from the trees the dry leaves fell
With a sad sound unspeakable.   160
The air was cold; till from the South
A gust blew hot, like sudden drouth,
Into their faces; and a light
Glowing and red, shone thro' the night.

A mighty city full of flame
And death and sounds without a name.
Amid the black and blinding smoke,
The people, as one man, awoke.
Oh! happy they who yesterday
On the long journey went away;   170
Whose pallid lips, smiling and chill,
While the flames scorch them smile on still;
Who murmur not; who tremble not
When the bier crackles fiery hot;
Who, dying, said in love's increase:
"Lord, let thy servant part in peace."

Those in the town could see and hear
A shaded river flowing near;
The broad deep bed could hardly hold
Its plenteous waters calm and cold.   180
Was flame-wrapped all the city wall,
The city gates were flame-wrapped all.

What was man's strength, what puissance then?

Christina Rossetti/99

Women were mighty as strong men.
Some knelt in prayer, believing still,
Resigned unto a righteous will,
Bowing beneath the chastening rod,
Lost to the world, but found of God.
Some prayed for friend, for child, for wife;
Some prayed for faith; some prayed for life;   190
While some, proud even in death, hope gone,
Steadfast and still, stood looking on.

"Death—death—oh! let us fly from death;
Where'er we go it followeth;
All these are dead; and we alone
Remain to weep for what is gone.
What is this thing? thus hurriedly
To pass into eternity;
To leave the earth so full of mirth;
To lose the profit of our birth;   200
To die and be no more; to cease,
Having numbness that is not peace.
Let us go hence; and, even if thus
Death everywhere must go with us,
Let us not see the change, but see
Those who have been or still shall be."

He sighed and they went on together;
Beneath their feet did the grass wither;
Across the heaven high overhead
Dark misty clouds floated and fled;   210
And in their bosom was the thunder,
And angry lightnings flashed out under,
Forked and red and menacing;
Far off the wind was muttering;
It seemed to tell, not understood,
Strange secrets to the listening wood.

Upon its wings it bore the scent
Of blood of a great armament:
Then saw they how on either side

Fields were down-trodden far and wide.
That morning at the break of day
Two nations had gone forth to slay.

As a man soweth so he reaps.
The field was full of bleeding heaps;
Ghastly corpses of men and horses
That met death at a thousand sources;
Cold limbs and putrifying flesh;
Long love-locks clotted to a mesh
That stifled; stiffened mouths beneath
Staring eyes that had looked on death.

But these were dead: these felt no more
The anguish of the wounds they bore.
Behold, they shall not sigh again,
Nor justly fear, nor hope in vain.

What if none wept above them?—is
The sleeper less at rest for this?
Is not the young child's slumber sweet
When no man watcheth over it?
These had deep calm; but all around
There was a deadly smothered sound,
The choking cry of agony
From wounded men who could not die;
Who watched the black wing of the raven
Rise like a cloud 'twixt them and heaven,
And in the distance flying fast
Beheld the eagle come at last.

She knelt down in her agony:
"O Lord, it is enough," said she:
"My heart's prayer putteth me to shame;
"Let me return to whence I came.
"Thou who for love's sake didst reprove,
"Forgive me for the sake of love."

SWEET DEATH*

The sweetest blossoms die.
And so it was that, going day by day
Unto the church to praise and pray,
And crossing the green church-yard thoughtfully,
I saw how on the graves the flowers
Shed their fresh leaves in showers;
And how their perfume rose up to the sky
Before it passed away.

The youngest blossoms die.
They die, and fall, and nourish the rich earth   10
From which they lately had their birth.
Sweet life: but sweeter death that passeth by,
And is as tho' it had not been.
All colors turn to green:
The bright hues vanish, and the odours fly;
The grass hath lasting worth.

And youth and beauty die.
So be it, O my God, thou God of truth.
Better than beauty and than youth
Are saints and angels, a glad company: 20
And Thou, O Lord, our Rest and Ease,
Art better far than these.
Why should we shrink from our full harvest? why
Prefer to glean with Ruth?

THE P.R.B.

The two Rossettis (brothers they)
And Holman Hunt and John Millais,
With Stephens chivalrous and bland,
And Woolner in a distant land—
In these six men I awestruck see
Embodied the great P.R.B.

* Published in *The Germ*.

D. G. Rossetti offered two
Good pictures to the public view;
Unnumbered ones great John Millais,
And Holman more than I can say.

William Rossetti, calm and solemn,
Cuts up his brethren by the column.

SONG*

Oh! roses for the flush of youth,
   And laurel for the perfect prime;
But pluck an ivy-branch for me,
   Grown old before my time.

Oh! violets for the grave of youth,
   And bay for those dead in their prime;
Give me the withered leaves I chose
   Before in the old time.

   * Published in *The Germ*.

HER FIRST SEASON*

He gazed her over, from her eyebrows down
    Even to her feet: he gazed so with the good
    Undoubting faith of fools, much as who should
  Accost God for a comrade. In the brown
Of all her curls he seemed to think the town
    Would make an acquisition; but her hood
    Was not the newest fashion, and his brood
Of lady-friends might scarce approve her gown.
If I did smile, 'twas faintly; for my cheeks
  Burned, thinking she'd be shown up to be sold,
  And cried about, in the thick jostling run
Of the loud world, till all the weary weeks
  Should bring her back to herself and to the old
Familiar face of nature and the sun.

CORDELIA*

    "The jewels of our father, with washed eyes
    Cordelia leaves you. I know you what you are
    And, like a sister, am most loth to tell
    Your faults, as they are named. Use well our father:
    To your professed bosoms I commit him.
    But yet, alas!—stood I within his grace,
    I would prefer him to a better place.
    So farewell to you both."

Cordelia, unabashed and strong,
  Her voice's quiet scarcely less
Than yester-eve, enduring wrong
And curses of her father's tongue,
  Departs, a righteous-souled princess;
Bidding her sisters cherish him.

    * Published in *The Germ.*

They turn on her and fix their eyes,
    But cease not passing inward;—one
Sneering with lips still curled to lies,
Sinuous of body, serpent-wise;   10
    Her footfall creeps, and her looks shun
The very thing on which they dwell.

The other, proud, with heavy cheeks
    And massive forehead, where remains
A mark of frowning. If she seeks
With smiles to tame her eyes, or speaks,
    Her mouth grows wanton: she disdains
The ground with haughty, measured steps.

The silent years had grown between
    Father and daughter. Always she   20
Had waited on his will, and been
Foremost in doing it,—unseen
    Often: she wished him not to see,
But served him for his sake alone.

He saw her constant love; and, tho'
    Occasion surely was not scant,
Perhaps had never sought to know
How she could give it wording. So
    His love, not stumbling at a want,
Among the three preferred her first.   30

Her's is the soul not stubborn, yet
    Asserting self. The heart was rich;
But, questioned, she had rather let
Men judge her conscious of a debt
    Than freely giving: thus, her speech
Is love according to her bond.

In France the queen Cordelia had
    Her hours well satisfied with love:
She loved her king, too, and was glad:
And yet, at times, a something sad,   40

May be, was with her, thinking of
The manner of his life at home.

But this does not usurp her mind.
    It is but sorrow guessed from far
Thro' twilight dimly. She must find
Her duty elsewhere: not resigned—
    Because she knows them what they are,
Yet scarcely ruffled from her peace.

Cordelia—a name well revered;
    Synonymous with truth and tried   50
Affection; which but needs be heard
To raise one selfsame thought endeared
    To men and women far and wide;
A name our mothers taught to us.

Like placid faces which you knew
    Years since, but not again shall meet;
On a sick bed like wind that blew;
An excellent thing, best likened to
    Her own voice, gentle, soft, and sweet;
SHAKESPEARE'S CORDELIA;—better thus.   60

TO THE CASTLE RAMPARTS *

The Castle is erect on the hill's top,
To moulder there all day and night: it stands
With the long shadow lying at its foot.
That is a weary height which you must climb
Before you reach it; and a dizziness
Turns in your eyes when you look down from it,
So standing clearly up into the sky.

I rose one day, having a mind to see it.
'Twas on a clear Spring morning, and a blackbird

    * Published in *The Germ*.

Awoke me with his warbling near my window: 10
My dream had fashioned this into a song
That some one with grey eyes was singing me,
And which had drawn me so into myself
That all the other shapes of sleep were gone:
And then, at last, it woke me, as I said.
The sun shone fully in on me; and brisk
Cool airs, that had been cold but for his warmth,
Blew thro' the open casement, and sweet smells
Of flowers with the dew yet fresh upon them,—
Rose-buds, and showery lilacs, and what stayed 20
Of April wallflowers.

                    I set early forth,
Wishing to reach the Castle when the heat
Should weigh upon it, vertical at noon.
My path lay thro' green open fields at first,
With now and then trees rising statelily
Out of the grass; and afterwards came lanes
Closed in by hedges smelling of the May,
And overshadowed by the meeting trees.
So I walked on with none but pleasant thoughts; 30
The Spring was in me, not alone around me,
And smiles came rippling o'er my lips for nothing.
I reached at length,—issuing from a lane
Which wound so that it seemed about to end
Always, yet ended not for a long while,—
A space of ground thick grassed and level to
The overhanging sky and the strong sun:
Before me the brown sultry hill stood out,
Peaked by its rooted Castle, like a part
Of its own self. I laid me in the grass, 40
Turning from it, and looking on the sky,
And listening to the humming in the air
That hums when no sound is; because I chose
To gaze on that which I had left, not that
Which I had yet to see. As one who strives
After some knowledge known not till he sought,
Whose soul acquaints him that his step by step

Has led him to a few steps next the end,
Which he foresees already, waits a little
Before he passes onward, gathering 50
Together in his thoughts what he has done.

Rising after a while, the ascent began.
Broken and bare the soil was; and thin grass,
Dry and scarce green, was scattered here and there
In tufts: and, toiling up, my knees almost
Reaching my chin, one hand upon my knee,
Or grasping sometimes at the earth, I went,
With eyes fixed on the next step to be taken,
Not glancing right or left; till, at the end,
I stood straight up, and the tower stood straight up 60
Before my face. One tower, and nothing more;
For all the rest has gone this way and that,
And is not anywhere, saving a few
Fragments that lie about, some on the top,
Some fallen half down on either side the hill,
Uncared for, well nigh grown into the ground.
The tower is grey, and brown, and black, with green
Patches of mildew and of ivy woven
Over the sightless loopholes and the sides:
And from the ivy deaf-coiled spiders dangle, 70
Or scurry to catch food; and their fine webs
Touch at your face wherever you may pass.
The sun's light scorched upon it; and a fry
Of insects in one spot quivered for ever,
Out and in, in and out, with glancing wings
That caught the light, and buzzings here and there;
That little life which swarms about large death;
No one too many or too few, but each
Ordained, and being each in its own place.
The ancient door, cut deep into the wall, 80
And cramped with iron rusty now and rotten,
Was open half: and, when I strove to move it
That I might have free passage inwards, stood
Unmoved and creaking with old uselessness:
So, pushing it, I entered, while the dust

Was shaken down upon me from all sides.
The narrow stairs, lighted by scanty streaks
That poured in thro' the loopholes pierced high up,
Wound with the winding tower, until I gained,
Delivered from the closeness and the damp   90
And the dim air, the outer battlements.

There opposite, the tower's black turret-girth
Suppressed the multiplied steep chasm of fathoms,
So that immediately the fields far down
Lay to their heaving distance for the eyes,
Satisfied with one gaze unconsciously,
To pass to glory of heaven, and to know light.
Here was no need of thinking:—merely sense
Was found sufficient: the wind made me free,
Breathed, and returned by me in a hard breath: 100
And what at first seemed silence, being roused
By callings of the cuckoo from far off,
Resolved itself into a sound of trees
That swayed, and into chirps reciprocal
On each side, and revolving drone of flies.
Then, stepping to the brink, and looking sheer
To where the slope ceased in the level stretch
Of country, I sat down to lay my head
Backwards into a single ivy-bush
Complex of leaf. I lay there till the wind   110
Blew to me, from a church seen miles away,
Half the hour's chimes.

                Great clouds were arched abroad
Like angels' wings; returning beneath which,
I lingered homewards. All their forms had merged
And loosened when my walk was ended; and,
While yet I saw the sun a perfect disc,
There was the moon beginning in the sky.

FANCIES AT LEISURE *

I. NOON REST

Following the river's course,
　　We come to where the sedges plant
Their thickest twinings at its source;—
　　A spot that makes the heart to pant,
Feeling its rest and beauty. Pull
The reeds' top thro' your fingers; dull
Your sense of the world's life; and toss
The thought away of hap or cross:
Then shall the river seem to call
Your name, and the slow quiet crawl　　　　　　　10
Between your eyelids like a swoon;
And all the sounds at heat of noon
And all the silence shall so sing
Your eyes asleep as that no wing
Of bird in rustling by, no prone
Willow-branch on your hair, no drone
Droning about and past you,—nought
May soon avail to rouse you, caught
With sleep thro' heat in the sun's light,—
So good, tho' losing sound and sight,　　　　　　　20
You scarce would waken, if you might.

II. A QUIET PLACE

My friend, are not the grasses here as tall
As you would wish to see? The runnell's fall
Over the rise of pebbles, and its blink
Of shining points which, upon this side, sink
In dark, yet still are there; this ragged crane
Spreading his wings at seeing us with vain
Terror, forsooth; the trees, a pulpy stock
Of toadstools huddled round them; and the flock—
Black wings after black wings—of ancient rook
By rook; has not the whole scene got a look　　　　　　　10

* Published in *The Germ*.

As tho' we were the first whose breath should fan
In two this spider's web, to give a span
Of life more to three flies? See, there's a stone
Seems made for us to sit on. Have men gone
By here, and passed? or rested on that bank
Or on this stone, yet seen no cause to thank
For the grass growing here so green and rank?

III. A FALL OF RAIN

It was at day-break my thought said:
"The moon makes chequered chestnut-shade
There by the south-side where the vine
Grapples the wall; and if it shine
This evening thro' the boughs and leaves,
And if the wind with silence weaves
More silence than itself, each stalk
Of flower just swayed by it, we'll walk,
Mary and I, when every fowl
Hides beak and eyes in breast, the owl   10
Only awake to hoot."—But clover
Is beaten down now, and birds hover,
Peering for shelter round; no blade
Of grass stands sharp and tall; men wade
Thro' mire with frequent plashing sting
Of rain upon their faces. Sing,
Then, Mary, to me thro' the dark:
But kiss me first: my hand shall mark
Time, pressing your's the while I hark.

IV. SHEER WASTE

Is it a little thing to lie down here
   Beside the water, looking into it,
    And see there grass and fallen leaves interknit,
    And small fish sometimes passing thro' some bit
Of tangled grass where there's an outlet clear?

And then a drift of wind perhaps will come,

And blow the insects hovering all about
  Into the water. Some of them get out;
  Others swim with sharp twitches; and you doubt
Whether of life or death for other some.   10

Meanwhile the blueflies sway themselves along
  Over the water's surface, or close by;
  Not one in ten beyond the grass will fly
  That closely skirts the stream; nor will your eye
Meet any where the sunshine is not strong.

After a time you find, you know not how,
  That it is quite a stretch of energy
  To do what you have done unconsciously,—
  That is, pull up the grass; and then you see
You may as well rise and be going now.   20

So, having walked for a few steps, you fall
  Bodily on the grass under the sun,
  And listen to the rustle, one by one,
  Of the trees' leaves; and soon the wind has done
For a short space, and it is quiet all;

Except because the rooks will make a caw
  Just now and then together: and the breeze
  Soon rises up again among the trees,
  Making the grass, moreover, bend and tease
Your face, but pleasantly. Mayhap the paw   30

Of a dog touches you and makes you rise
  Upon one arm to pat him; and he licks
  Your hand for that. A child is throwing sticks,
  Hard by, at some half-dozen cows, which fix
Upon him their unmoved contented eyes.

The sun's heat now is painful. Scarce can you
  Move, and even less lie still. You shuffle then,
  Poised on your arms, again to shade. Again
  There comes a pleasant laxness on you. When
You have done enough of nothing, you will go.   40

Some hours perhaps have passed. Say not you fling
   These hours or such-like recklessly away.
   Seeing the grass and sun and children, say,
   Is not this something more than idle play,
Than careless waste? Is it a little thing?

V. IN SPRING

The sky is blue here, scarcely with a stain
   Of grey for clouds: here the young grasses gain
   A larger growth of green over this splinter
   Fallen from the ruin. Spring seems to have told Winter
He shall not freeze again here. Tho' their loss
Of leaves is not yet quite repaired, trees toss
Sprouts from their boughs. The ash you called so stiff
Curves, daily, broader shadow down the cliff.

VI. IN SUMMER

How the rooks caw, and their beaks seem to clank!
   Let us just move out there,—(it might be cool
Under those trees,) and watch how the thick tank
   By the old mill is black,—a stagnant pool
Of rot and insects. There goes by a lank
   Dead hairy dog floating. Will Nature's rule
Of life return hither no more? The plank
   Rots in the crushed weeds, and the sun is cruel.

VII. THE BREADTH OF NOON

Long time I lay there, while a breeze would blow
   From the south softly, and, hard by, a slender
   Poplar swayed to and fro to it. Surrender
Was made of all myself to quiet. No
Least thought was in my mind of the least woe:
   Yet the void silence slowly seemed to render
   My calmness not less calm, but yet more tender,
And I was nigh to weeping.—'Ere I go,'
I thought, 'I must make all this stillness mine;

The sky's blue almost purple, and these three
Hills carved against it, and the pine on pine
   The wood in their shade has. All this I see
   So inwardly I fancy it may be
Seen thus of parted souls by *their* sunshine.'

VIII. SEA-FRESHNESS

Look at that crab there. See if you can't haul
   His backward progress to this spar of a ship
   Thrown up and sunk into the sand here. Clip
His clipping feelers hard, and give him all
Your hand to gripe at: he'll take care not fall:
   So,—but with heed, for you are like to slip
   In stepping on the plank's sea-slime. Your lip—
No wonder—curves in mirth at the slow drawl
Of the squat creature's legs. We've quite a shine
   Of waves round us, and here there comes a wind
   So fresh it must bode us good luck. How long
Boatman, for one and sixpence? Line by line
   The sea comes toward us sun-ridged. Oh! we sinned
   Taking the crab out: let's redress his wrong.

IX. THE FIRE SMOULDERING

I look into the burning coals, and see
   Faces and forms of things; but they soon pass,
   Melting one into other: the firm mass
Crumbles, and breaks, and fades gradually,
Shape into shape as in a dream may be,
   Into an image other than it was:
   And so on till the whole falls in, and has
Not any likeness,—face, and hand, and tree,
All gone. So with the mind: thought follows thought,
   This hastening, and that pressing upon this,
   A mighty crowd within so narrow room:
   And then at length heavy-eyed slumbers come,
   The drowsy fancies grope about, and miss
Their way, and what was so alive is nought.

"JESUS WEPT"

Mary rose up, as one in sleep might rise,
    And went to meet her brother's Friend: and they
    Who tarried with her said: "she goes to pray
And weep where her dead brother's body lies."
So, with their wringing of hands and with sighs,
They stood before Him in the public way.
"Had'st Thou been with him, Lord, upon that day,
He had not died," she said, drooping her eyes.
Mary and Martha with bowed faces kept
    Holding His garments, one on each side.—"Where
      Have ye laid him?" He asked. "Lord, come and see."—
    The sound of grieving voices heavily
    And universally was round Him there,
A sound that smote His spirit. Jesus wept.

FROM *The Earthly Paradise*

THE SINGER'S PRELUDE

Of Heaven or Hell I have no power to sing,
  I cannot ease the burden of your fears,
Or make quick-coming death a little thing,
Or bring again the pleasure of past years,
Nor for my words shall ye forget your tears,
Or hope again for aught that I can say,
The idle singer of an empty day.

  But rather, when aweary of your mirth
From full hearts still unsatisfied ye sigh,
And, feeling kindly unto all the earth,   10
Grudge every minute as it passes by,
Made the more mindful that the sweet days die.—
Remember me a little then, I pray,
The idle singer of an empty day.

  The heavy trouble, the bewildering care
That weighs us down who live and earn our bread,
These idle verses have no power to bear;
So let me sing of names remembered,
Because they, living not, can ne'er be dead,
Or long time take their memory quite away   20
From us poor singers of an empty day.

  Dreamer of dreams, born out of my due time,
Why should I strive to set the crooked straight?
Let it suffice me that my murmuring rhyme
Beats with light wing against the ivory gate,
Telling a tale not too importunate
To those who in the sleepy region stay,
Lull'd by the singer of an empty day.

Folk say, a wizard to a northern king
At Christmas-tide such wondrous things did show,   30
That through one window men beheld the spring,
And through another saw the summer glow,
And through a third the fruited vines a-row,
While still, unheard, but in its wonted way,
Pip'd the drear wind of that December day.

So with this Earthly Paradise it is,
If ye will read aright, and pardon me,
Who strive to build a shadowy isle of bliss
Midmost the beating of the steely sea,
Where toss'd about all hearts of men must be;   40
Whose ravening monsters mighty men shall slay,
Not the poor singer of an empty day.

THE KING'S VISIT

So long he rode he drew anigh
A mill upon the river's brim,
That seem'd a goodly place to him,
For o'er the oily smooth millhead
There hung the apples growing red,
And many an ancient apple-tree
Within the orchard could he see,
While the smooth millwalls white and black
Shook to the great wheel's measur'd clack,
And grumble of the gear within;   10
While o'er the roof that dull'd that din
The doves sat crooning half the day,
And round the half-cut stack of hay
The sparrows flutter'd twittering.
There smiling stay'd the joyous king,
And since the autumn noon was hot
Thought good anigh that pleasant spot
To dine that day, and therewith sent
To tell the miller his intent:
Who held the stirrup of the king,   20

Bareheaded, joyful at the thing,
While from his horse he lit adown,
Then led him o'er an elm-beam brown,
New cut in February tide,
That cross'd the stream from side to side;
So underneath the apple trees
The king sat careless, well at ease,
And ate and drank right merrily.
    To whom the miller drew anigh
Among the courtiers, bringing there   30
Such as he could of country fare,
Green yellowing plums from off his wall,
Wasp-bitten pears, the first to fall
From off the wavering spire-like tree,
Junkets, and cream and fresh honey.

FROM *The Life and Death of Jason*

A GARDEN BY THE SEA

I know a little garden close
Set thick with lily and red rose,
Where I would wander if I might
From dewy dawn to dewy night,
And have one with me wandering.

And though within it no birds sing,
And though no pillared house is there,
And though the apple boughs are bare
Of fruit and blossom, would to God
Her feet upon the green grass trod,   10
And I beheld them as before.

There comes a murmur from the shore,
And in the close two fair streams are,
Drawn from the purple hills afar,
Drawn down unto the restless sea—

Dark hills whose heath-bloom feeds no bee,
Dark shore no ship has ever seen,
Still beaten by the billows green,
Whose murmur comes unceasingly
Unto the place for which I cry.   20

For which I cry both day and night,
For which I let slip all delight,
Whereby I grow both deaf and blind,
Careless to win, unskilled to find,
And quick to lose what all men seek.

Yet tottering as I am, and weak,
Still have I left a little breath
To seek within the jaws of death
An entrance to that happy place,
To seek the unforgotten face,   30
Once seen, once kissed, once reft from me
Anigh the murmuring of the sea.

THE BLUE CLOSET [1]

THE DAMOZELS

Lady Alice, Lady Louise,
Between the wash of the tumbling seas
We are ready to sing, if so ye please;
So lay your long hands on the keys;
        Sing, *"Laudate pueri."*

And ever the great bell overhead
Boomed in the wind a knell for the dead,
Though no one tolled it, a knell for the dead.

[1] Morris wrote this poem about a painting by Dante Gabriel
Rossetti. Lady Louise's lover, Lord Arthur, had gone away,
and now she and Lady Alice and the Damozels are meeting
on Christmas Eve to pray. In her dreams at these prayers,
Lord Arthur appears to Lady Louise.

Sister, let the measure swell
Not too loud; for you sing not well   10
If you drown the faint boom of the bell;
        He is weary, so am I.

And ever the chevron overhead
Flapped on the banner of the dead.
(Was he asleep, or was he dead?)

LADY ALICE

Alice the Queen, and Louise the Queen,
Two damozels wearing purple and green,
Four lone ladies dwelling here
From day to day and year to year;
And there is none to let us go;   20
To break the locks of the doors below,
Or shovel away the heaped-up snow;
And when we die no man will know
That we are dead; but they give us leave,
Once every year on Christmas Eve,
To sing in the Closet Blue one song;
And we should be so long, so long,
If we dared, in singing; for dream on dream,
They float on in a happy stream;
Float from the gold strings, float from the keys,   30
Float from the opened lips of Louise;
But, alas! the sea-salt oozes through
The chinks of the tiles of the Closet Blue;

And ever the great bell overhead
Booms in the wind a knell for the dead,
The wind plays on it a knell for the dead.

        [*They sing all together.*]

How long ago was it, how long ago,
He came to this tower with hands full of snow?

"Kneel down, O love Louise, kneel down," he said,
And sprinkled the dusty snow over my head.   40

He watched the snow melting, it ran through my hair,
Ran over my shoulders, white shoulders and bare.

"I cannot weep for thee, poor love Louise,
For my tears are all hidden deep under the seas;

"In a gold and blue casket she keeps all my tears,
But my eyes are no longer blue, as in old years;

"Yea, they grow gray with time, grow small and dry;
I am so feeble now, would I might die."

And in truth the great bell overhead
Left off his pealing for the dead,   50
Perchance, because the wind was dead.

Will he come back again, or is he dead?
Oh! is he sleeping, my scarf round his head?

Or did they strangle him as he lay there,
With the long scarlet scarf I used to wear?

Only I pray thee, Lord, let him come here!
Both his soul and his body to me are most dear.

Dear Lord, that loves me, I wait to receive
Either body or spirit this wild Christmas Eve.

Through the floor shot up a lily red,   60
With a patch of earth from the land of the dead,
For he was strong in the land of the dead.

What matter that his cheeks were pale,
    His kind kissed lips all gray?
"O love Louise, have you waited long?"
    "O my lord Arthur, yea."

What if his hair that brushed her cheek
 Was stiff with frozen rime?
His eyes were grown quite blue again,
 As in the happy time.

"O love Louise, this is the key
 Of the happy golden land!
O sisters, cross the bridge with me,
 My eyes are full of sand.
What matter that I cannot see,
 If ye take me by the hand?"

And ever the great bell overhead,
And the tumbling seas mourned for the dead;
For their song ceased, and they were dead.

THE DEFENCE OF GUENEVERE

But, knowing now that they would have her speak,
She threw her wet hair backward from her brow,
Her hand close to her mouth touching her cheek,

As though she had had there a shameful blow,
And feeling it shameful to feel aught but shame
All through her heart, yet felt her cheek burned so,

She must a little touch it; like one lame
She walked away from Gauwaine, with her head
Still lifted up; and on her cheek of flame

The tears dried quick; she stopped at last and said: 10
"O knights and lords, it seems but little skill
To talk of well-known things past now and dead.

"God wot I ought to say, I have done ill,
And pray you all forgiveness heartily!
Because you must be right, such great lords; still

"Listen—suppose your time were come to die,
And you were quite alone and very weak;
Yea, laid a-dying, while very mightily

"The wind was ruffling up the narrow streak
Of river through your broad lands running well;   20
Suppose a hush should come, then someone speak:

" 'One of these cloths is heaven, and one is hell;
Now choose one cloth forever—which they be,
I will not tell you; you must somehow tell

" 'Of your own strength and mightiness; here, see!'
Yea, yea, my lord, and you to ope your eyes,
At foot of your familiar bed to see

"A great God's angel standing, with such dyes,
Not known on earth, on his great wings, and hands,
Held out two ways, light from the inner skies   30

"Showing him well, and making his commands
Seem to be God's commands, moreover, too,
Holding within his hands the cloths on wands;

"And one of these strange choosing cloths was blue,
Wavy and long, and one cut short and red;
No man could tell the better of the two.

"After a shivering half-hour you said:
'God help! heaven's color, the blue'; and he said, 'hell.'
Perhaps you would then roll upon your bed,

"And cry to all good men that loved you well,   40
'Ah, Christ! if only I had known, known, known';
Launcelot went away, then I could tell,

"Like wisest man how all things would be, moan,
And roll and hurt myself, and long to die,
And yet fear much to die for what was sown.

"Nevertheless, you, O Sir Gauwaine, lie;
Whatever may have happened through these years,
God knows I speak truth, saying that you lie."

Her voice was low at first, being full of tears,
But as it cleared, it grew full loud and shrill,   50
Growing a windy shriek in all men's ears,

A ringing in their startled brains, until
She said that Gauwaine lied, then her voice sunk,
And her great eyes began again to fill,

Though still she stood right up, and never shrunk,
But spoke on bravely, glorious lady fair!
Whatever tears her full lips may have drunk,

She stood, and seemed to think, and wrung her hair,
Spoke out at last with no more trace of shame,
With passionate twisting of her body there: 60

"It chanced upon a day that Launcelot came
To dwell at Arthur's court—at Christmas-time
This happened; when the heralds sung his name,

"Son of King Ban of Benwick, seemed to chime
Along with all the bells that rang that day,
O'er the white roofs, with little change of rime.

"Christmas and whitened winter passed away,
And over me the April sunshine came,
Made very awful with black hail-clouds; yea,

"And in the summer I grew white with flame,   70
And bowed my head down; autumn, and the sick
Sure knowledge things would never be the same,

"However often spring might be most thick
Of blossoms and buds, smote on me, and I grew
Careless of most things, let the clock tick, tick,

"To my unhappy pulse, that beat right through
My eager body; while I laughed out loud,
And let my lips curl up at false or true,

"Seemed cold and shallow without any cloud.
Behold, my judges, then the cloths were brought;   80
While I was dizzied thus, old thoughts would crowd,

"Belonging to the time ere I was bought
By Arthur's great name and his little love;
Must I give up forever then, I thought,

"That which I deemed would ever round me move
Glorifying all things; for a little word,
Scarce ever meant at all, must I now prove

"Stone-cold forever? Pray you, does the Lord
Will that all folks should be quite happy and good?
I love God now a little, if this cord   90

"Were broken, once for all what striving could
Make me love anything in earth or heaven?
So day by day it grew, as if one should

"Slip slowly down some path worn smooth and even,
Down to a cool sea on a summer day;
Yet still in slipping there was some small leaven

"Of stretched hands catching small stones by the way,
Until one surely reached the sea at last,
And felt strange new joy as the worn head lay

"Back, with the hair like sea-weed; yea, all past   100
Sweat of the forehead, dryness of the lips,
Washed utterly out by the dear waves o'ercast,

"In the lone sea, far off from any ships!
Do I not know now of a day in spring?
No minute of that wild day ever slips

"From out my memory; I hear thrushes sing,
And wheresoever I may be, straightway
Thoughts of it all come up with most fresh sting.

"I was half mad with beauty on that day,
And went, without my ladies, all alone,   110
In a quiet garden walled round every way;

"I was right joyful of that wall of stone,
That shut the flowers and trees up with the sky,
And trebled all the beauty; to the bone—

"Yea, right through to my heart, grown very shy
With wary thoughts—it pierced, and made me glad,
Exceedingly glad, and I knew verily,

"A little thing just then had made me mad;
I dared not think, as I was wont to do,
Sometimes, upon my beauty; if I had   120

"Held out my long hand up against the blue,
And, looking on the tenderly darkened fingers,
Thought that by rights one ought to see quite through,

"There, see you, where the soft still light yet lingers,
Round by the edges; what should I have done,
If this had joined with yellow spotted singers,

"And startling green drawn upward by the sun?
But shouting, loosed out, see now! all my hair,
And trancedly stood watching the west wind run

"With faintest half-heard breathing sound—why there   130
I lose my head e'en now in doing this.
But shortly listen: In that garden fair

"Came Launcelot walking; this is true, the kiss
Wherewith we kissed in meeting that spring day,
I scarce dare talk of the remembered bliss,

"When both our mouths went wandering in one way,
And aching sorely, met among the leaves;
Our hands, being left behind, strained far away.

"Never within a yard of my bright sleeves
Had Launcelot come before—and now so nigh!   140
After that day why is it Guenevere grieves?

"Nevertheless, you, O Sir Gauwaine, lie,
Whatever happened on through all those years—
God knows I speak truth, saying that you lie.

"Being such a lady, could I weep these tears
If this were true? A great queen such as I,
Having sinned this way, straight her conscience sears;

"And afterwards she liveth hatefully,
Slaying and poisoning—certes never weeps;
Gauwaine, be friends now, speak me lovingly.   150

"Do I not see how God's dear pity creeps
All through your frame, and trembles in your mouth?
Remember in what grave your mother sleeps,

"Buried in some place far down in the south,
Men are forgetting as I speak to you;
By her head, severed in that awful drouth

"Of pity that drew Agravaine's fell blow,
I pray your pity! let me not scream out
Forever after, when the shrill winds blow

"Through half your castle-locks! let me not shout   160
Forever after in the winter night
When you ride out alone! in battle-rout

"Let not my rusting tears make your sword light!
Ah! God of mercy, how he turns away!
So, ever must I dress me to the fight,

"So—let God's justice work! Gauwaine, I say,
See me hew down your proofs; yea, all men know,
Even as you said, how Mellyagraunce one day,

"One bitter day in *la Fausse Garde*, for so   170
All good knights held it after, saw—
Yea, sirs, by cursed unknightly outrage, though

"You, Gauwaine, held his word without a flaw,
This Mellyagraunce saw blood upon my bed—
Whose blood then pray you? is there any law

"To make a queen say why some spots of red
Lie on her coverlet, or will you say,
'Your hands are white, lady, as when you wed,

" 'Where did you bleed?' and must I stammer out—'Nay,
I blush indeed, fair lord, only to rend
My sleeve up to my shoulder, where there lay   180

" 'A knife-point last night': so must I defend
The honor of the Lady Guenevere?
Not so, fair lords, even if the world should end

"This very day, and you were judges here
Instead of God. Did you see Mellyagraunce
When Launcelot stood by him?—what white fear

"Curled his blood, and how his teeth did dance,
His side sink in? as my knight cried and said:
'Slayer of unarmed men, here is a chance!

" 'Setter of traps, I pray you guard your head;   190
By God, I am so glad to fight with you,
Stripper of ladies, that my hand feels lead

" 'For driving weight; hurrah now! draw and do,
For all my wounds are moving in my breast,
And I am getting mad with waiting so.'

"He struck his hands together o'er the beast,
Who fell down flat, and groveled at his feet,
And groaned at being slain so young. 'At least,'

"My knight said, 'Rise you, sir, who are so fleet
At catching ladies; half-armed will I fight,   200
My left side all uncovered!' Then, I weet,

"Up sprang Sir Mellyagraunce with great delight
Upon his knave's face; not until just then
Did I quite hate him, as I saw my knight

"Along the lists look to my stake and pen
With such a joyous smile, it made me sigh
From agony beneath my waist-chain, when

"The fight began, and to me they drew nigh;
Ever Sir Launcelot kept him on the right,
And traversed warily, and ever high   210

"And fast leapt caitiff's sword, until my knight
Sudden threw up his sword to his left hand,
Caught it, and swung it; that was all the fight,

"Except a spout of blood on the hot land;
For it was hottest summer; and I know
I wondered how the fire, while I should stand,

"And burn, against the heat, would quiver so,
Yards above my head; thus these matters went;
Which things were only warnings of the woe

"That fell on me. Yet Mellyagraunce was shent,   220
For Mellyagraunce had fought against the Lord;
Therefore, my lords, take heed lest you be blent

"With all his wickedness—say no rash word
Against me, being so beautiful; my eyes,
Wept all away to gray, may bring some sword

"To drown you in your blood; see my breast rise,
Like waves of purple sea, as here I stand;
And how my arms are moved in wonderful wise;

"Yea, also at my full heart's strong command,
See through my long throat how the words go up   230
In ripples to my mouth; how in my hand

"The shadow lies like wine within a cup
Of marvelously colored gold; yea, now
This little wind is rising, look you up,

"And wonder how the light is falling so
Within my moving tresses. Will you dare
When you have looked a little on my brow,

"To say this thing is vile? or will you care
For any plausible lies of cunning woof,
When you can see my face with no lie there   240

"Forever? Am I not a gracious proof?—
'But in your chamber Launcelot was found'—
Is there a good knight then would stand aloft,

"When a queen says with gentle queenly sound,
'O true as steel, come now and talk with me;
I love to see your step upon the ground

" 'Unwavering; also well I love to see
That gracious smile light up your face, and hear
Your wonderful words, that all mean verily

" 'The thing they seem to mean. Good friend, so dear   250
To me in everything, come here tonight,
Or else the hours will pass most dull and drear.

" 'If you come not, I fear this time I might
Get thinking overmuch of times gone by,
When I was young, and green hope was in sight;

" 'For no man cares now to know why I sigh;
And no man comes to sing me pleasant songs,
Nor any brings me the sweet flowers that lie

" 'So thick in the gardens, therefore one so longs
To see you, Launcelot, that we may be   260
Like children once again, free from all wrongs

" 'Just for one night.' Did he not come to me?
What thing could keep true Launcelot away
If I said, 'Come'? There was one less than three

"In my quiet room that night, and we were gay;
Till sudden I rose up, weak, pale, and sick,
Because a bawling broke our dream up; yea,

"I looked at Launcelot's face and could not speak,
For he looked helpless, too, for a little while;
Then I remember how I tried to shriek,   270

"And could not, but fell down; from tile to tile
The stones they threw up rattled o'er my head
And made me dizzier; till within a while

"My maids were all about me, and my head
On Launcelot's breast was being soothed away
From its white chattering, until Launcelot said . . .

"By God! I will not tell you more today—
Judge any way you will; what matters it?
You know quite well the story of that fray,

"How Launcelot stilled their bawling, the mad fit   280
That caught up Gauwaine, all, all, verily,
But just that which would save me; these things flit.

"Nevertheless, you, O Sir Gauwaine, lie;
Whatever may have happened these long years,
God knows I speak truth, saying that you lie!

"All I have said is truth, by Christ's dear tears."
She would not speak another word, but stood   ,
Turned sideways, listening, like a man who hears

His brother's trumpet sounding through the wood
Of his foes' lances. She leaned eagerly,   290
And gave a slight spring sometimes, as she could

At last hear something really; joyfully
Her cheek grew crimson, as the headlong speed
Of the roan charger drew all men to see,
The knight who came was Launcelot at good need.

THE HAYSTACK IN THE FLOODS

Had she come all the way for this,
To part at last without a kiss?
Yea, had she borne the dirt and rain
That her own eyes might see him slain
Beside the haystack in the floods?

Along the dripping, leafless woods,
The stirrup touching either shoe,
She rode astride as troopers do;
With kirtle kilted to her knee,
To which the mud splashed wretchedly;   10
And the wet dripped from every tree
Upon her head and heavy hair,
And on her eyelids broad and fair;
The tears and rain ran down her face.

By fits and starts they rode apace,
And very often was his place
Far off from her; he had to ride
Ahead, to see what might betide
When the roads crossed; and sometimes, when
There rose a murmuring from his men,   20

Had to turn back with promises.
Ah me! she had but little ease;
And often for pure doubt and dread
She sobbed, made giddy in the head
By the swift riding; while, for cold,
Her slender fingers scarce could hold
The wet reins; yea, and scarcely, too,
She felt the foot within her shoe
Against the stirrup; all for this,
To part at last without a kiss   30
Beside the haystack in the floods.

For when they neared that old soaked hay,
They saw across the only way
That Judas, Godmar, and the three
Red running lions dismally
Grinned from his pennon, under which
In one straight line along the ditch,
They counted thirty heads.
                    So then
While Robert turned round to his men,
She saw at once the wretched end,   40
And, stooping down, tried hard to rend
Her coif the wrong way from her head,
And hid her eyes; while Robert said,
"Nay, love, 'tis scarcely two to one;
At Poictiers where we made them run
So fast—why, sweet my love, good cheer,
The Gascon frontier is so near,
Naught after us."
                    But "O!" she said,
"My God! my God! I have to tread
The long way back without you; then   50
The court at Paris; those six men;
The gratings of the Chatelet;
The swift Seine on some rainy day
Like this, and people standing by,
And laughing, while my weak hands try
To recollect how strong men swim.

All this, or else a life with him,
For which I should be damned at last;
Would God that this next hour were past!"

He answered not, but cried his cry,   60
"St. George for Marny!" cheerily;
And laid his hand upon her rein.
Alas! no man of all his train
Gave back that cheery cry again;
And, while for rage his thumb beat fast
Upon his sword-hilt, someone cast
About his neck a kerchief long,
And bound him.

     Then they went along
To Godmar; who said: "Now, Jehane,
Your lover's life is on the wane   70
So fast, that, if this very hour
You yield not as my paramour,
He will not see the rain leave off;
Nay, keep your tongue from gibe and scoff,
Sir Robert, or I slay you now."

She laid her hand upon her brow,
Then gazed upon the palm, as though
She thought her forehead bled, and "No!"
She said, and turned her head away,
As there was nothing else to say,   80
And everything was settled; red
Grew Godmar's face from chin to head—
"Jehane, on yonder hill there stands
My castle, guarding well my lands;
What hinders me from taking you,
And doing that I list to do
To your fair willful body, while
Your knight lies dead?"

     A wicked smile
Wrinkled her face, her lips grew thin,

A long way out she thrust her chin:
"You know that I should strangle you
While you were sleeping; or bite through
Your throat, by God's help; ah!" she said,
"Lord Jesus, pity your poor maid!
For in such wise they hem me in,
I cannot choose but sin and sin,
Whatever happens; yet I think
They could not make me eat or drink,
And so should I just reach my rest."

"Nay, if you do not my behest,
O Jehane! though I love you well,"
Said Godmar, "would I fail to tell
All that I know?" "Foul lies," she said.
"Eh? lies, my Jehane? by God's head,
At Paris folks would deem them true!
Do you know, Jehane, they cry for you:
'Jehane the brown! Jehane the brown!
Give us Jehane to burn or drown!
Eh!—gag me Robert!—sweet my friend,
This were indeed a piteous end
For those long fingers, and long feet,
And long neck, and smooth shoulders sweet;
An end that few men would forget
That saw it. So, an hour yet—
Consider, Jehane, which to take
Of life or death!"

      So, scarce awake,
Dismounting, did she leave that place,
And totter some yards; with her face
Turned upward to the sky she lay,
Her head on a wet heap of hay,
And fell asleep; and while she slept,
And did not dream, the minutes crept
Round to the twelve again; but she,
Being waked at last, sighed quietly,
And strangely childlike came, and said:
"I will not." Straightway Godmar's head,

As though it hung on strong wires, turned
Most sharply round, and his face burned.

For Robert, both his eyes were dry—
He could not weep—but gloomily   130
He seemed to watch the rain; yea, too,
His lips were firm; he tried once more
To touch her lips; she reached out, sore,
And vain desire so tortured them,
The poor gray lips, and now the hem
Of his sleeve brushed them.

      With a start
Up Godmar rose, thrust them apart;
From Robert's throat he loosed the bands
Of silk and mail; with empty hands
Held out, she stood and gazed, and saw,   140
The long bright blade without a flaw
Glide out from Godmar's sheath, his hand
In Robert's hair; she saw him bend
Back Robert's head; she saw him send
The thin steel down; the blow told well—
Right backward the knight Robert fell,
And moaned as dogs do, being half dead,
Unwitting, as I deem; so then
Godmar turned grinning to his men,
Who ran, some five or six, and beat   150
His head to pieces at their feet.

Then Godmar turned again and said:
"So, Jehane, the first fitte is read!
Take note, my lady, that your way
Lies backward to the Chatelet!"
She shook her head and gazed awhile
At her cold hands with a rueful smile,
As though this thing had made her mad.

This was the parting that they had
Beside the haystack in the floods.   160

THE SAILING OF THE SWORD

Across the empty garden-beds,
  When the Sword went out to sea,
I scarcely saw my sisters' heads
  Bowed each beside a tree.
I could not see the castle-leads,
  When the Sword went out to sea.

Alicia wore a scarlet gown,
  When the Sword went out to sea,
But Ursula's was russet brown;
  For the mist we could not see   10
The scarlet roofs of the good town,
  When the Sword went out to sea.

Green holly in Alicia's hand,
  When the Sword went out to sea;
With sear oak-leaves did Ursula stand;
  O! yet alas for me!
I did but bear a peeled white wand,
  When the Sword went out to sea.

Oh, russet brown and scarlet bright,
  When the Sword went out to sea,   20
My sisters wore; I wore but white.
  Red, brown, and white are three;
Three damozels; each had a knight,
  When the Sword went out to sea.

Sir Robert shouted loud, and said,
  When the Sword went out to sea,
"Alicia, while I see thy head,
  What shall I bring for thee?"
"Oh, my sweet lord, a ruby red—"
  The Sword went out to sea.   30

Sir Miles said, while the sails hung down,
  When the Sword went out to sea,

"Oh, Ursula! while I see the town,
  What shall I bring for thee?"
"Dear knight, bring back a falcon brown"—
  The Sword went out to sea.

But my Roland, no word he said
  When the Sword went out to sea,
But only turned away his head—
  A quick shriek came from me: 40
"Come back, dear lord, to your white maid"—
  The Sword went out to sea.

The hot sun bit the garden-beds,
  When the Sword came back from sea;
Beneath an apple-tree our heads
  Stretched out toward the sea;
Gray gleamed the thirsty castle-leads,
  When the Sword came back from sea.

Lord Robert brought a ruby red,
  When the Sword came back from sea;   50
He kissed Alicia on the head—
  "I am come back to thee;
'Tis time, sweet love, that we were wed,
  Now the Sword is back from sea!"

Sir Miles he bore a falcon brown,
  When the Sword came back from sea;
His arms went round tall Ursula's gown—
  "What joy, O love, but thee?
Let us be wed in the good town,
  Now the Sword is back from sea!"   60

My heart grew sick, no more afraid,
  When the Sword came back from sea;
Upon the deck a tall white maid
  Sat on Lord Roland's knee;
His chin was pressed upon her head,
  When the Sword came back from sea!

138/*William Morris*

THE GILLYFLOWER OF GOLD

A golden gillyflower today
I wore upon my helm alway,
And won the prize of this tourney.
  Hah! hah! la belle jaune giroflée.

However well Sir Giles might sit,
His sun was weak to wither it;
Lord Miles's blood was dew on it.
  Hah! hah! la belle jaune giroflée.

Although my spear in splinters flew,
From John's steel-coat, my eye was true;   10
I wheeled about, and cried for you,
  Hah! hah! la belle jaune giroflée.

Yea, do not doubt my heart was good,
Though my sword flew like rotten wood,
To shout, although I scarcely stood,
  Hah! hah! la belle jaune giroflée.

My hand was steady too, to take
My ax from round my neck, and break
John's steel-coat up for my love's sake.
  Hah! hah! la belle jaune giroflée—   20

When I stood in my tent again,
Arming afresh, I felt a pain
Take hold of me, I was so fain—
  Hah! hah! la belle jaune giroflée—

To hear *Honneur aux fils des preux!*
Right in my ears again, and shew
The gillyflower blossomed new.
  Hah! hah! la belle jaune giroflée.

The Sieur Guillaume against me came,
His tabard bore three points of flame   30

From a red heart; with little blame—
  Hah! hah! la belle jaune giroflée—

Our tough spears crackled up like straw;
He was the first to turn and draw
His sword, that had nor speck nor flaw;
  Hah! hah! la belle jaune giroflée.

But I felt weaker than a maid,
And my brain, dizzied and afraid,
Within my helm a fierce tune played,
  Hah hah! la belle jaune giroflée,   40

Until I thought of your dear head,
Bowed to the gillyflower bed,
The yellow flowers stained with red;
  Hah! hah! la belle jaune giroflée.

Crash! how the swords met—*giroflée!*
The fierce tune in my helm would play,
La belle! la belle! jaune giroflée!
  Hah! hah! la belle jaune giroflée.

Once more the great swords met again;
"*La belle! la belle!*" but who fell then?   50
Le Sieur Guillaume, who struck down ten;
  Hah! hah! la belle jaune giroflée.

And as with mazed and unarmed face
Toward my own crown and the Queen's place,
They led me at a gentle pace—
  Hah! hah! la belle jaune giroflée—

I almost saw your quiet head
Bowed o'er the gillyflower bed,
The yellow flowers stained with red.
  Hah! hah! la belle jaune giroflée.

DOLORES

NOTRE-DAME DES SEPT DOULEURS

Cold eyelids that hide like a jewel
    Hard eyes that grow soft for an hour;
The heavy white limbs, and the cruel
    Red mouth like a venomous flower;
When these are gone by with their glories,
    What shall rest of thee then, what remain,
O mystic and somber Dolores,
    Our Lady of Pain?

Seven sorrows the priests give their Virgin;
    But thy sins, which are seventy times seven,   10
Seven ages would fail thee to purge in,
    And then they would haunt thee in heaven:
Fierce midnights and famishing morrows,
    And the loves that complete and control
All the joys of the flesh, all the sorrows
    That wear out the soul.

O garment not golden but gilded,
    O garden where all men may dwell,
O tower not of ivory, but builded
    By hands that reach heaven from hell;   20
O mystical rose of the mire,
    O house not of gold but of gain,
O house of unquenchable fire,
    Our Lady of Pain!

O lips full of lust and of laughter,
    Curled snakes that are fed from my breast,
Bite hard, lest remembrance come after
    And press with new lips where you pressed.

For my heart too springs up at the pressure,
   Mine eyelids too moisten and burn;   30
Ah, feed me and fill me with pleasure,
   Ere pain come in turn.

In yesterday's reach and tomorrow's,
   Out of sight though they lie of today,
There have been and there yet shall be sorrows
   That smite not and bite not in play.
The life and the love thou despisest,
   These hurt us indeed, and in vain,
O wise among women, and wisest,
   Our Lady of Pain.   40

Who gave thee thy wisdom? what stories
   That stung thee, what visions that smote?
Wert thou pure and a maiden, Dolores,
   When desire took thee first by the throat?
What bud was the shell of a blossom
   That all men may smell to and pluck?
What milk fed thee first at what bosom?
   What sins gave thee suck?

We shift and bedeck and bedrape us,
   Thou art noble and nude and antique;   50
Libitina thy mother, Priapus
   Thy father, a Tuscan and Greek.
We play with light loves in the portal,
   And wince and relent and refrain;
Loves die, and we know thee immortal,
   Our Lady of Pain.

Fruits fail and love dies and time ranges;
   Thou art fed with perpetual breath,
And alive after infinite changes,
   And fresh from the kisses of death;   60
Of languors rekindled and rallied,
   Of barren delights and unclean,
Things monstrous and fruitless, a pallid
   And poisonous queen.

Could you hurt me, sweet lips, though I hurt you?
    Men touch them, and change in a trice
The lilies and languors of virtue
    For the raptures and roses of vice;
Those lie where thy foot on the floor is,
    These crown and caress thee and chain,   70
O splendid and sterile Dolores,
    Our Lady of Pain.

There are sins it may be to discover,
    There are deeds it may be to delight.
What new work wilt thou find for thy lover,
    What new passions for daytime or night?
What spells that they know not a word of
    Whose lives are as leaves overblown?
What tortures undreamt of, unheard of,
    Unwritten, unknown?   80

Ah, beautiful passionate body
    That never has ached with a heart!
On thy mouth though the kisses are bloody,
    Though they sting till it shudder and smart,
More kind than the love we adore is,
    They hurt not the heart or the brain,
O bitter and tender Dolores,
    Our Lady of Pain.

As our kisses relax and redouble,
    From the lips and the foam and the fangs   90
Shall no new sin be born for men's trouble,
    No dream of impossible pangs?
With the sweet of the sins of old ages
    Wilt thou satiate thy soul as of yore?
Too sweet is the rind, say the sages,
    Too bitter the core.

Hast thou told all thy secrets the last time,
    And bared all thy beauties to one?
Ah, where shall we go then for pastime,

If the worst that can be has been done? 100
But sweet as the rind was the core is;
   We are fain of thee still, we are fain,
O sanguine and subtle Dolores,
   Our Lady of Pain.

By the hunger of change and emotion,
   By the thirst of unbearable things,
By despair, the twin-born of devotion,
   By the pleasure that winces and stings,
The delight that consumes the desire,
   The desire that outruns the delight, 110
By the cruelty deaf as a fire
   And blind as the night,

By the ravenous teeth that have smitten
   Through the kisses that blossom and bud,
By the lips intertwisted and bitten
   Till the foam has a savor of blood,
By the pulse as it rises and falters,
   By the hands as they slacken and strain,
I adjure thee, respond from thine altars,
   Our Lady of Pain. 120

Wilt thou smile as a woman disdaining
   The light fire in the veins of a boy?
But he comes to thee sad, without feigning,
   Who has wearied of sorrow and joy;
Less careful of labor and glory
   Than the elders whose hair has uncurled;
And young, but with fancies as hoary
   And gray as the world.

I have passed from the outermost portal
   To the shrine where a sin is a prayer; 130
What care though the service be mortal?
   O our Lady of Torture, what care?
All thine the last wine that I pour is,
   The last in the chalice we drain,

O fierce and luxurious Dolores,
    Our Lady of Pain.

All thine the new wine of desire,
    The fruit of four lips as they clung
Till the hair and the eyelids took fire,
    The foam of a serpentine tongue,   140
The froth of the serpents of pleasure,
    More salt than the foam of the sea,
Now felt as a flame, now at leisure
    As wine shed for me.

Ah, thy people, thy children, thy chosen,
    Marked cross from the womb and perverse!
They have found out the secret to cozen
    The gods that constrain us and curse;
They alone, they are wise, and none other;
    Give me place, even me, in their train,   150
O my sister, my spouse, and my mother,
    Our Lady of Pain.

For the crown of our life as it closes
    Is darkness, the fruit thereof dust;
No thorns go as deep as a rose's,
    And love is more cruel than lust.
Time turns the old days to derision,
    Our loves into corpses or wives;
And marriage and death and division
    Make barren our lives.   160

And pale from the past we draw nigh thee,
    And satiate with comfortless hours;
And we know thee, how all men belie thee,
    And we gather the fruit of thy flowers;
The passion that slays and recovers,
    The pangs and the kisses that rain
On the lips and the limbs of thy lovers,
    Our Lady of Pain.

Algernon Charles Swinburne/145

The desire of thy furious embraces
    Is more than the wisdom of years,   170
On the blossom though blood lie in traces,
    Though the foliage be sodden with tears.
For the lords in whose keeping the door is
    That opens on all who draw breath
Gave the cypress to love, my Dolores,
    The myrtle to death.

And they laughed, changing hands in the measure,
    And they mixed and made peace after strife;
Pain melted in tears, and was pleasure;
    Death tingled with blool, and was life.   180
Like lovers they melted and tingled,
    In the dusk of thine innermost fane;
In the darkness they murmured and mingled,
    Our Lady of Pain.

In a twilight where virtues are vices,
    In thy chapels, unknown of the sun,
To a tune that enthralls and entices,
    They were wed, and the twain were as one.
For the tune from thine altar hath sounded
    Since God bade the world's work begin,   190
And the fume of thine incense abounded,
    To sweeten the sin.

Love listens, and paler than ashes,
    Through his curls as the crown on them slips,
Lifts languid wet eyelids and lashes,
    And laughs with insatiable lips.
Thou shalt hush him with heavy caresses,
    With music that scares the profane;
Thou shalt darken his eyes with thy tresses,
    Our Lady of Pain.   200

Thou shalt blind his bright eyes though he wrestle,
    Thou shalt chain his light limbs though he strive;
In his lips all thy serpents shall nestle,

In his hands all thy cruelties thrive.
In the daytime thy voice shall go through him,
    In his dreams he shall feel thee and ache;
Thou shalt kindle by night and subdue him
    Asleep and awake.

Thou shalt touch and make redder his roses
    With juice not of fruit nor of bud;   210
When the sense in the spirit reposes,
    Thou shalt quicken the soul through the blood.
Thine, thine the one grace we implore is,
    Who would live and not languish or feign,
O sleepless and deadly Dolores,
    Our Lady of Pain.

Dost thou dream, in a respite of slumber,
    In a lull of the fires of thy life,
Of the days without name, without number,
    When thy will stung the world into strife;   220
When, a goddess, the pulse of thy passion
    Smote kings as they reveled in Rome;
And they hailed thee re-risen, O Thalassian,
    Foam-white, from the foam?

When thy lips had such lovers to flatter;
    When the city lay red from thy rods,
And thine hands were as arrows to scatter
    The children of change and their gods;
When the blood of thy foemen made fervent
    A sand never moist from the main,   230
As one smote them, their lord and thy servant,
    Our Lady of Pain.

On sands by the storm never shaken,
    Nor wet from the washing of tides;
Nor by foam of the waves overtaken,
    Nor winds that the thunder bestrides;
But red from the print of thy paces,
    Made smooth for the world and its lords,

Ringed round with a flame of fair faces,
  And splendid with swords.   240

There the gladiator, pale for thy pleasure,
  Drew bitter and perilous breath;
There torments laid hold on the treasure
  Of limbs too delicious for death;
When thy gardens were lit with live torches;
  When the world was a steed for thy rein;
When the nations lay prone in thy porches,
  Our Lady of Pain.

When, with flame all around him aspirant,
  Stood flushed, as a harp-player stands,   250
The implacable beautiful tyrant,
  Rose-crowned, having death in his hands;
And a sound as the sound of loud water
  Smote far through the flight of the fires,
And mixed with the lightning of slaughter
  A thunder of lyres.

Dost thou dream of what was and no more is,
  The old kingdoms of earth and the kings?
Dost thou hunger for these things, Dolores,
  For these, in a world of new things?   260
But thy bosom no fasts could emaciate,
  No hunger compel to complain
Those lips that no bloodshed could satiate,
  Our Lady of Pain.

As of old when the world's heart was lighter,
  Through thy garments the grace of thee glows,
The white wealth of thy body made whiter
  By the blushes of amorous blows,
And seamed with sharp lips and fierce fingers,
  And branded by kisses that bruise;   270
When all shall be gone that now lingers,
  Ah, what shall we lose?

Thou wert fair in the fearless old fashion,
    And thy limbs are as melodies yet,
And move to the music of passion
    With lithe and lascivious regret.
What ailed us, O gods, to desert you
    For creeds that refuse and restrain?
Come down and redeem us from virtue,
    Our Lady of Pain.   280

All shrines that were Vestal are flameless,
    But the flame has not fallen from this;
Though obscure be the god, and though nameless
    The eyes and the hair that we kiss;
Low fires that love sits by and forges
    Fresh heads for his arrows and thine;
Hair loosened and soiled in mid orgies
    With kisses and wine.

The skin changes country and color,
    And shrivels or swells to a snake's.   290
Let it brighten and bloat and grow duller,
    We know it, the flames and the flakes,
Red brands on it smitten and bitten,
    Round skies where a star is a stain,
And the leaves with their litanies written,
    Our Lady of Pain.

On thy bosom though many a kiss be,
    There are none such as knew it of old.
Was it Alciphron once or Arisbe,
    Male ringlets or feminine gold,   300
That thy lips met with under the statue,
    Whence a look shot out sharp after thieves
From the eyes of the garden god at you
    Across the fig-leaves?

Then still, through dry seasons and moister,
    One god had a wreath to his shrine;
Then love was the pearl of his oyster,

And Venus rose red out of wine.
We have all done amiss, choosing rather
   Such loves as the wise gods disdain;   310
Intercede for us thou with thy father,
   Our Lady of Pain.

In spring he had crowns of his garden,
   Red corn in the heat of the year,
Then hoary green olives that harden
   When the grape-blossom freezes with fear;
And milk-budded myrtles with Venus
   And vine-leaves with Bacchus he trod;
And ye said, "We have seen, he hath seen us,
   A visible god."   320

What broke off the garlands that girt you?
   What sundered you spirit and clay?
Weak sins yet alive are as virtue
   To the strength of the sins of that day.
For dried is the blood of thy lover,
   Ipsithilla, contracted the vein;
Cry aloud, "Will he rise and recover,
   Our Lady of Pain?"

Cry aloud; for the old world is broken.
   Cry out; for the Phrygian is priest,   330
And rears not the bountiful token
   And spreads not the fatherly feast.
From the midmost of Ida, from shady
   Recesses that murmur at morn,
They have brought and baptized her, Our Lady,
   A goddess new-born.

And the chaplets of old are above us,
   And the oyster-bed teems out of reach;
Old poets outsing and outlove us,
   And Catullus makes mouths at our speech.   340
Who shall kiss, in thy father's own city,
   With such lips as he sang with, again?

Intercede for us all of thy pity,
    Our Lady of Pain.

Out of Dindymus heavily laden
    Her lions draw bound and unfed
A mother, a mortal, a maiden,
    A queen over death and the dead.
She is cold, and her habit is lowly,
    Her temple of branches and sods;   350
Most fruitful and virginal, holy,
    A mother of gods.

She hath wasted with fire thine high places,
    She hath hidden and marred and made sad
The fair limbs of the Loves, the fair faces
    Of gods that were goodly and glad.
She slays, and her hands are not bloody;
    She moves as a moon in the wane,
White-robed, and thy raiment is ruddy,
    Our Lady of Pain.   360

They shall pass and their places be taken,
    The gods and the priests that are pure.
They shall pass, and shalt thou not be shaken?
    They shall perish, and shalt thou endure?
Death laughs, breathing close and relentless
    In the nostrils and eyelids of lust,
With a pinch in his fingers of scentless
    And delicate dust.

But the worm shall revive thee with kisses;
    Thou shalt change and transmute as a god,   370
As the rod to a serpent that hisses,
    As the serpent again to a rod.
Thy life shall not cease though thou doff it;
    Thou shalt live until evil be slain,
And good shall die first, said thy prophet,
    Our Lady of Pain.

Algernon Charles Swinburne/151

Did he lie? did he laugh? does he know it,
   Now he lies out of reach, out of breath,
Thy prophet, thy preacher, thy poet,
   Sin's child by incestuous Death? 380
Did he find out in fire at his waking,
   Or discern as his eyelids lost light,
When the bands of the body were breaking
   And all came in sight?

Who has known all the evil before us,
   Or the tyrannous secrets of time?
Though we match not the dead men that bore us
   At a song, at a kiss, at a crime—
Though the heathen outface and outlive us,
   And our lives and our longings are twain— 390
Ah, forgive us our virtues, forgive us,
   Our Lady of Pain.

Who are we that embalm and embrace thee
   With spices and savors of song?
What is time, that his children should face thee?
   What am I, that my lips do thee wrong?
I could hurt thee—but pain would delight thee;
   Or caress thee—but love would repel;
And the lovers whose lips would excite thee
   Are serpents in hell. 400

Who now shall content thee as they did,
   Thy lovers, when temples were built
And the hair of the sacrifice braided
   And the blood of the sacrifice spilt,
In Lampsacus fervent with faces,
   In Aphaca red from thy reign,
Who embraced thee with awful embraces,
   Our Lady of Pain?

Where are they, Cotytto or Venus,
   Astarte or Ashtaroth, where? 410
Do their hands as we touch come between us?

Is the breath of them hot in thy hair?
From their lips have thy lips taken fever,
    With the blood of their bodies grown red?
Hast thou left upon earth a believer
    If these men are dead?

They were purple of raiment and golden,
    Filled full of thee, fiery with wine,
Thy lovers, in haunts unbeholden,
    In marvelous chambers of thine.   420
They are fled, and their footprints escape us,
    Who appraise thee, adore, and abstain,
O daughter of Death and Priapus,
    Our Lady of Pain.

What ails us to fear overmeasure,
    To praise thee with timorous breath,
O mistress and mother of pleasure,
    The one thing as certain as death?
We shall change as the things that we cherish,
    Shall fade as they faded before,   430
As foam upon water shall perish,
    As sand upon shore.

We shall know what the darkness discovers,
    If the grave-pit be shallow or deep;
And our fathers of old, and our lovers,
    We shall know if they sleep not or sleep.
We shall see whether hell be not heaven,
    Find out whether tares be not grain,
And the joys of thee seventy times seven,
    Our Lady of Pain.   440

OCTOPUS

by Algernon Charles Sin-Burne [1]

Strange beauty, eight-limbed and eight-handed,
  Whence camest to dazzle our eyes?
With thy bosom bespangled and banded
  With the hues of the seas and the skies;
Is thy home European or Asian,
  O mystical monster marine?
Part molluscous and partly crustacean,
  Betwixt and between.

Wast thou born to the sound of sea trumpets,
  Hast thou eaten and drunk to excess   10
Of the sponges—thy muffins and crumpets,
  Of the seaweed—thy mustard and cress?
Wast thou nurtured in caverns of coral,
  Remote from reproof or restraint?
Art thou innocent, art thou immoral,
  Sinburnian or saint?

Lithe limbs, curling free, as a creeper
  That creeps in a desolate place,
To enroll and envelop the sleeper
  In a silent and stealthy embrace,   20
Cruel beak craning forward to bite us,
  Our juices to drain and to drink,
Or to whelm us in waves of Cocytus,
  Indelible ink!

[1] This poem, while not absolutely justifiable in this collection, is such a splendid parody of Swinburne's "Dolores" that it is included to illustrate at least one kind of reaction to the "fleshly school of poetry." It was published in 1872.

O breast, that 'twere rapture to writhe on!
  O arms 'twere delicious to feel
Clinging close with the crush of the Python,
  When she maketh her murderous meal!
In thy eight-fold embraces enfolden,
  Let our empty existence escape;   30
Give us death that is glorious and golden,
  Crushed all out of shape!

Ah! thy lips, lascivious and luscious,
  With death in their amorous kiss,
Cling round us, and clasp us, and crush us,
  With bitings of agonized bliss;
We are sick with the poison of pleasure,
  Dispense us the potion of pain;
Ope thy mouth to its uttermost measure
  And bite us again!   40

DEDICATION TO *Poems and Ballads* [1]

The sea gives her shells to the shingle,
    The earth gives her streams to the sea;
They are many, but my gift is single,
    My verses, the first fruits of me.
Let the wind take the green and the gray leaf,
    Cast forth without fruit upon air;
Take rose-leaf and vine-leaf and bay-leaf
    Blown loose from the hair.

The night shakes them round me in legions,
    Dawn drives them before her like dreams;   10
Time sheds them like snows on strange regions,
    Swept shoreward on infinite streams;
Leaves pallid and somber and ruddy,
    Dead fruits of the fugitive years;
Some stained as with wine and made bloody,
    And some as with tears.

Some scattered in seven years' traces,
    As they fell from the boy that was then;
Long left among idle green places,
    Or gathered but now among men;   20
On seas full of wonder and peril,
    Blown white round the capes of the north;
Or in islands where myrtles are sterile
    And loves bring not forth.

O daughters of dreams and of stories
    That life is not wearied of yet,
Faustine, Fragoletta, Dolores,

[1] The dedication is addressed to Edward Burne-Jones (later
Sir Edward), one of the Pre-Raphaelite painters. The volume
Poems and Ballads set off the controversy about the "fleshly"
quality of Pre-Raphaelite art.

Félise and Yolande and Juliette,
Shall I find you not still, shall I miss you,
    When sleep, that is true or that seems,   30
Comes back to me hopeless to kiss you,
    O daughters of dreams?

They are past as a slumber that passes,
    As the dew of a dawn of old time;
More frail than the shadows on glasses,
    More fleet than a wave or a rime.
As the waves after ebb drawing seaward,
    When their hollows are full of the night,
So the birds that flew singing to me-ward
    Recede out of sight.   40

The songs of dead seasons, that wander
    On wings of articulate words;
Lost leaves that the shore-wind may squander,
    Light flocks of untameable birds;
Some sang to me dreaming in class time
    And truant in hand as in tongue;
For the youngest were born of boy's pastime,
    The eldest are young.

Is there shelter while life in them lingers,
    Is there hearing for songs that recede,   50
Tunes touched from a harp with man's fingers
    Or blown with boy's mouth in a reed?
Is there place in the land of your labor,
    Is there room in your world of delight,
Where change has not sorrow for neighbor
    And day has not night?

In their wings though the sea-wind yet quivers,
    Will you spare not a space for them there
Made green with the running of rivers
    And gracious with temperate air;   60
In the fields and the turreted cities,
    That cover from sunshine and rain

Fair passions and bountiful pities
    And loves without stain?

In a land of clear colors and stories,
    In a region of shadowless hours,
Where earth has a garment of glories
    And a murmur of musical flowers;
In woods where the spring half uncovers
    The flush of her amorous face,   70
By the waters that listen for lovers,
    For these is there place?

For the song-birds of sorrow, that muffle
    Their music as clouds do their fire;
For the storm-birds of passion, that ruffle
    Wild wings in a wind of desire;
In the stream of the storm as it settles
    Blown seaward, borne far from the sun,
Shaken loose on the darkness like petals
    Dropped one after one?   80

Though the world of your hands be more gracious
    And lovelier in lordship of things
Clothed round by sweet art with the spacious
    Warm heaven of her imminent wings,
Let them enter, unfledged and nigh fainting,
    For the love of old loves and lost times;
And receive in your palace of painting
    This revel of rimes.

Though the seasons of man full of losses
    Make empty the years full of youth,   90
If but one thing be constant in crosses,
    Change lays not her hand upon truth;
Hopes die, and their tombs are for token
    That the grief as the joy of them ends
Ere time that breaks all men has broken
    The faith between friends.

Though the many lights dwindle to one light,
    There is help if the heaven has one;
Though the skies be discrowned of the sunlight
    And the earth dispossessed of the sun,   100
They have moonlight and sleep for repayment,
    When, refreshed as a bride and set free,
With stars and sea-winds in her raiment,
    Night sinks on the sea.

THE GARDEN OF PROSERPINE

Here, where the world is quiet;
    Here, where all trouble seems
Dead winds' and spent waves' riot
    In doubtful dreams of dreams;
I watch the green field growing
For reaping folk and sowing,
For harvest-time and mowing,
    A sleepy world of streams.

I am tired of tears and laughter,
    And men that laugh and weep,   10
Of what may come hereafter
    For men that sow to reap;
I am weary of days and hours,
Blown buds of barren flowers,
Desires and dreams and powers
    And everything but sleep.

Here life has death for neighbor,
    And far from eye or ear
Wan waves and wet winds labor,
    Weak ships and spirits steer;   20
They drive adrift, and whither
They wot not who make thither;
But no such winds blow hither,
    And no such things grow here.

No growth of moor or coppice,
   No heather-flower or vine,
But bloomless buds of poppies,
   Green grapes of Proserpine,
Pale beds of blowing rushes
Where no leaf blooms or blushes   30
Save this whereout she crushes
   For dead men deadly wine.

Pale, without name or number,
   In fruitless fields of corn,
They bow themselves and slumber
   All night till light is born;
And like a soul belated,
In hell and heaven unmated,
By cloud and mist abated
   Comes out of darkness morn.   40

Though one were strong as seven,
   He too with death shall dwell,
Nor wake with wings in heaven,
   Nor weep for pains in hell;
Though one were fair as roses,
His beauty clouds and closes;
And well though love reposes,
   In the end it is not well.

Pale, beyond porch and portal,
   Crowned with calm leaves, she stands   50
Who gathers all things mortal
   With cold immortal hands;
Her languid lips are sweeter
Than love's who fears to greet her
To men that mix and meet her
   From many times and lands.

She waits for each and other,
   She waits for all men born;
Forgets the earth her mother,
   The life of fruits and corn;   60

And spring and seed and swallow
Take wing for her and follow
Where summer song rings hollow
    And flowers are put to scorn.

There go the loves that wither,
    The old loves with wearier wings;
And all dead years draw thither,
    And all disastrous things;
Dead dreams of days forsaken,
Blind buds that snows have shaken,   70
Wild leaves that winds have taken,
    Red strays of ruined springs.

We are not sure of sorrow,
    And joy was never sure;
Today will die tomorrow;
    Time stoops to no man's lure;
And love, grown faint and fretful,
With lips but half regretful
Sighs, and with eyes forgetful
    Weeps that no loves endure.   80

From too much love of living,
    From hope and fear set free,
We thank with brief thanksgiving
    Whatever gods may be
That no life lives forever;
That dead men rise up never;
That even the weariest river
    Winds somewhere safe to sea.

Then star nor sun shall waken,
    Nor any change of light;   90
Nor sound of waters shaken,
    Nor any sound or sight;
Nor wintry leaves nor vernal,
Nor days nor things diurnal;
Only the sleep eternal
    In an eternal night.

Algernon Charles Swinburne/161

FROM *Atalanta in Calydon*

When the Hounds of Spring

When the hounds of spring are on winter's traces,
    The mother of months in meadow or plain
Fills the shadows and windy places
    With lisp of leaves and ripple of rain;
And the brown bright nightingale amorous
Is half assuaged for Itylus,
For the Thracian ships and the foreign faces,
    The tongueless vigil, and all the pain.

Come with bows bent and with emptying of quivers,
    Maiden most perfect, lady of light,   10
With a noise of winds and many rivers,
    With a clamor of waters, and with might;
Bind on thy sandals, O thou most fleet,
Over the splendor and speed of thy feet;
For the faint east quickens, the wan west shivers,
    Round the feet of the day and the feet of the night.

Where shall we find her, how shall we sing to her,
    Fold our hands round her knees, and cling?
Oh, that man's heart were as fire and could spring to her,
    Fire, or the strength of the streams that spring!   20
For the stars and the winds are unto her
As raiment, as songs of the harp-player;
For the risen stars and the fallen cling to her,
    And the southwest-wind and the west-wind sing.

For winter's rains and ruins are over,
    And all the season of snows and sins;
The days dividing lover and lover,
    The light that loses, the night that wins;
And time remembered is grief forgotten,
And frosts are slain and flowers begotten,   30
And in green underwood and cover
    Blossom by blossom the spring begins.

The full streams feed on flower of rushes,
   Ripe grasses trammel a traveling foot,
The faint fresh flame of the young year flushes
   From leaf to flower and flower to fruit;
And fruit and leaf are as gold and fire,
And the oat is heard above the lyre,
And the hooféd heel of a satyr crushes
   The chestnut-husk at the chestnut-root.   40

And Pan by noon and Bacchus by night,
   Fleeter of foot than the fleet-foot kid,
Follows with dancing and fills with delight
   The Maenad and the Bassarid;
And soft as lips that laugh and hide
The laughing leaves of the trees divide,
And screen from seeing and leave in sight
   The god pursuing, the maiden hid.

The ivy falls with the Bacchanal's hair
   Over her eyebrows hiding her eyes;   50
The wild vine slipping down leaves bare
   Her bright breast shortening into sighs;
The wild vine slips with the weight of its leaves,
But the berried ivy catches and cleaves
To the limbs that glitter, the feet that scare
   The wolf that follows, the fawn that flies.

HERTHA [1]

   I am that which began;
      Out of me the years roll;
      Out of me God and man;
   I am equal and whole;
God changes, and man, and the form of them bodily; I am
   the soul.

   [1] Hertha is the goddess of the earth and of fertility in ancient Germanic mythology.

Before ever land was,
Before ever the sea,
Or soft hair of the grass,
Or fair limbs of the tree,
Or the flesh-colored fruit of my branches, I was, and thy soul
was in me.   10

First life on my sources
First drifted and swam;
Out of me are the forces
That save it or damn;
Out of me man and woman, and wild-beast and bird; before
God was, I am.

Beside or above me
Naught is there to go;
Love or unlove me,
Unknow me or know,
I am that which unloves me and loves; I am stricken, and I
am the blow.   20

I the mark that is missed
And the arrows that miss,
I the mouth that is kissed
And the breath in the kiss,
The search, and the sought, and the seeker, the soul and the
body that is.

I am that thing which blesses
My spirit elate;
That which caresses
With hands uncreate
My limbs unbegotten that measure the length of the measure
of fate.   30

But what thing dost thou now,
Looking Godward, to cry,
"I am I, thou art thou,
I am low, thou art high"?

I am thou, whom thou seekest to find him; find thou but thy-
   self, thou art I.

      I the grain and the furrow,
         The plow-cloven clod
      And the plowshare drawn thorough,
         The germ and the sod,
The deed and the doer, the seed and the sower, the dust
   which is God.   40

      Hast thou known how I fashioned thee,
         Child, underground?
      Fire that impassioned thee,
         Iron that bound,
Dim changes of water, what thing of all these hast thou
   known of or found?

      Canst thou say in thine heart
         Thou has seen with thine eyes
      With what cunning of art
         Thou wast wrought in what wise,
By what force of what stuff thou wast shapen, and shown on
   my breast to the skies?   50

      Who hath given, who hath sold it thee,
         Knowledge of me?
      Hath the wilderness told it thee?
         Hast thou learnt of the sea?
Hast thou communed in spirit with night? Have the winds
   taken counsel with thee?

      Have I set such a star
         To show light on thy brow
      That thou sawest from afar
         What I show to thee now?
Have ye spoken as brethren together, the sun and the mountains and thou?   60

      What is here, dost thou know it?

                                    Algernon Charles Swinburne/165

What was, hast thou known?
    Prophet nor poet
    Nor tripod nor throne
Nor spirit nor flesh can make answer, but only thy mother
    alone.

    Mother, not maker,
        Born, and not made;
    Though her children forsake her,
        Allured or afraid,
Praying prayers to the God of their fashion, she stirs not for
    all that have prayed.   70

    A creed is a rod,
        And a crown is of night;
    But this thing is God,
        To be man with thy might,
To grow straight in the strength of thy spirit, and live out
    thy life as the light.

    I am in thee to save thee,
        As my soul in thee saith;
    Give thou as I gave thee,
        Thy life-blood and breath,
Green leaves of thy labor, white flowers of thy thought, and
    red fruit of thy death.   80

    Be the ways of thy giving
        As mine were to thee;
    The free life of thy living,
        Be the gift of it free;
Not as servant to lord, nor as master to slave, shalt thou give
    thee to me.

    O children of banishment,
        Souls overcast,
    Were the lights ye see vanish meant
        Alway to last,
Ye would know not the sun overshining the shadows and
    stars overpast.   90

166/*Algernon Charles Swinburne*

I that saw where ye trod
    The dim paths of the night
Set the shadow called God
    In your skies to give light;
But the morning of manhood is risen, and the shadowless
    soul is in sight.

The tree many-rooted [2]
    That swells to the sky
With frondage red-fruited,
    The life-tree am I;
In the buds of your lives is the sap of my leaves; ye shall live
    and not die.   100

But the gods of your fashion
    That take and that give,
In their pity and passion
    That scourge and forgive,
They are worms that are bred in the bark that falls off; they
    shall die and not live.

My own blood is what stanches
    The wounds in my bark;
Stars caught in my branches
    Make day of the dark,
And are worshiped as suns till the sunrise shall tread out their
    fires as a spark.   110

Where dead ages hide under
    The live roots of the tree,
In my darkness the thunder
    Makes utterance of me;
In the clash of my boughs with each other ye hear the waves
    sound of the sea.

That noise is of Time,
    As his feathers are spread

[2] The tree is Yggdrasill, the roots of which supported the
whole earth. Norse mythology.

And his feet set to climb
Through the boughs overhead,
And my foliage rings round him and rustles, and branches are
bent with his tread.   120

The storm-winds of ages
Blow through me and cease,
The war-wind that rages,
The spring-wind of peace,
Ere the breath of them roughen my tresses, ere one of my
blossoms increase.

All sounds of all changes,
All shadows and lights
On the world's mountain-ranges
And stream-riven heights,
Whose tongue is the wind's tongue and language of storm-
clouds on earth-shaking nights;   130

All forms of all faces,
All works of all hands
In unsearchable places
Of time-stricken lands,
All death and all life, and all reigns and all ruins, drop
through me as sands.

Though sore be my burden
And more than ye know,
And my growth have no guerdon
But only to grow,
Yet I fail not of growing for lightnings above me or death-
worms below.   140

These too have their part in me,
As I too in these;
Such fire is at heart in me,
Such sap is this tree's,
Which hath in it all sounds and all secrets of infinite lands
and of seas.

168/*Algernon Charles Swinburne*

In the spring-colored hours
        When my mind was as May's,
There brake forth of me flowers
        By centuries of days,
Strong blossoms with perfume of manhood, shot out from my
        spirit as rays.   150

And the sound if them springing
        And smell of their shoots
Were as warmth and sweet singing
        And strength to my roots;
And the lives of my children made perfect with freedom of
        soul were my fruits.

I bid you but be;
        I have need not of prayer;
I have need of you free
        As your mouths of mine air;
That my heart may be greater within me, beholding the fruits
        of me fair.   160

More fair than strange fruit is
        Of faiths ye espouse;
In me only the root is
        That blooms in your boughs;
Behold now your God that ye made you, to feed him with
        faith of your vows.

In the darkening and whitening
        Abysses adored,
With dayspring and lightning
        For lamp and for sword,
God thunders in heaven, and his angels are red with the
        wrath of the Lord.   170

O my sons, O too dutiful
        Toward gods not of me,
Was not I enough beautiful?
        Was it hard to be free?

For behold, I am with you, am in you and of you; look forth
now and see.

> Lo, winged with world's wonders,
>> With miracles shod,
> With the fires of his thunders
>> For raiment and rod,

God trembles in heaven, and his angels are white with the
terror of God.   180

> For his twilight is come on him,
>> His anguish is here;
> And his siprits gaze dumb on him,
>> Grown gray from his fear;

And his hour taketh hold on him stricken, the last of his
infinite year.

> Thought made him and breaks him,
>> Truth slays and forgives;
> But to you, as time takes him,
>> This new thing it gives,

Even love, the beloved Republic, that feeds upon freedom
and lives.   190

> For truth only is living,
>> Truth only is whole,
> And the love of his giving
>> Man's polestar and pole;

Man, pulse of my center, and fruit of my body, and seed of
my soul;

> One birth of my bosom;
>> One beam of mine eye;
> One topmost blossom
>> That scales the sky;

Man, equal and one with me, man that is made of me, man
that is I.   200

A FORSAKEN GARDEN

In a coign of the cliff between lowland and highland,
  At the sea-down's edge between windward and lee,
Walled round with rocks as an inland island,
  The ghost of a garden fronts the sea.
A girdle of brushwood and thorn encloses
  The steep square slope of the blossomless bed
Where the weeds that grew green from the graves of its roses
  Now lie dead.

The fields fall southward, abrupt and broken,
  To the low last edge of the long lone land.   10
If a step should sound or a word be spoken,
  Would a ghost not rise at the strange guest's hand?
So long have the gray bare walks lain guestless,
  Through branches and briars if a man make way,
He shall find no life, but the sea-wind's, restless
  Night and day.

The dense hard passage is blind and stifled
  That crawls by a track none turn to climb
To the strait waste place that the years have rifled
  Of all but the thorns that are touched not of time.   20
The thorns he spares when the rose is taken;
  The rocks are left when he wastes the plain.
The wind that wanders, the weeds windshaken,
  These remain.

Not a flower to be pressed of the foot that falls not;
  As the heart of a dead man the seed-plots are dry;
From the thicket of thorns whence the nightingale calls not,
  Could she call, there were never a rose to reply.
Over the meadows that blossom and wither
  Wings but the note of a sea-bird's song;   30
Only the sun and the rain come hither
  All year long.

The sun burns sear and the rain dishevels

One gaunt bleak blossom of scentless breath.
Only the wind here hovers and revels
  In a round where life seems barren as death.
Here there was laughing of old, there was weeping,
  Haply, of lovers none ever will know,
Whose eyes went seaward a hundred sleeping
  Years ago.   40

Heart handfast in heart as they stood, "Look thither,"
  Did he whisper? "look forth from the flowers to the sea;
For the foam-flowers endure when the rose-blossoms wither,
  And men that love lightly may die—but we?"
And the same wind sang and the same waves whitened,
  And or ever the garden's last petals were shed,
In the lips that had whispered, the eyes that had lightened,
  Love was dead.

Or they loved their life through, and then went whither?
  And were one to the end—but what end who knows?   50
Love deep as the sea as a rose must wither,
  As the rose-red seaweed that mocks the rose.
Shall the dead take thought for the dead to love them?
  What love was ever as deep as a grave?
They are loveless now as the grass above them
  Or the wave.

All are at one now, roses and lovers,
  Not known of the cliffs and the fields and the sea.
Not a breath of the time that has been hovers
  In the air now soft with a summer to be.   60
Not a breath shall there sweeten the seasons hereafter
  Of the flowers or the lovers that laugh now or weep,
When as they that are free now of weeping and laughter
  We shall sleep.

Here death may deal not again forever;
  Here change may come not till all change end.
From the graves they have made they shall rise up never,
  Who have left naught living to ravage and rend.

Earth, stones, and thorns of the wild ground growing,
    While the sun and the rain live, these shall be;   70
Till a last wind's breath upon all these blowing
    Roll the sea.

Till the slow sea rise and the sheer cliff crumble,
    Till terrace and meadow the deep gulfs drink,
Till the strength of the waves of the high tides humble
    The fields that lessen, the rocks that shrink,
Here now in his triumph where all things falter,
    Stretched out on the spoils that his own hand spread,
As a god self-slain on his own strange altar,
    Death lies dead.   80

MORNING SLEEP*

Another day hath dawned
Since, hastily and tired, I threw myself
Into the dark lap of advancing sleep.
Meanwhile through the oblivion of the night
The ponderous world its old course hath fulfilled,
And now the gradual sun begins to throw
Its slanting glory on the heads of trees,
And every bird stirs in its nest revealed,
And shakes its dewy wings.

          A blessed gift   10
Unto the weary hath been mine to-night,
Slumber unbroken: now it floats away:—
But whether 'twere not best to woo it still,
The head thus properly disposed, the eyes
In a continual dawning, mingling earth
And heaven with vagrant fantasies,—one hour,—
Yet for another hour? I will not break
The shining woof; I will not rudely leap
Out of this golden atmosphere, through which
I see the forms of immortalities.   20
Verily, soon enough the laboring day
With its necessitous unmusical calls
Will force the indolent conscience into life.

The uncouth moth upon the window-panes
Hath ceased to flap, or traverse with blind whirr
The room's dusk corners; and the leaves without
Vibrate upon their thin stems with the breeze
Flying towards the light. To an Eastern vale
That light may now be waning, and across

   * Published in *The Germ.*

The tall reeds by the Ganges, lotus-paved,
Lengthening the shadows of the banyan-tree.
The rice-fields are all silent in the glow,
All silent the deep heaven without a cloud,
Burning like molten gold. A red canoe
Crosses with fan-like paddles and the sound
Of feminine song, freighted with great-eyed maids
Whose unzoned bosoms swell on the rich air;
A lamp is in each hand; some mystic rite
Go they to try. Such rites the birds may see,
Ibis or emu, from their cocoa nooks,—
What time the granite sentinels that watch
The mouths of cavern-temples hail the first
Faint star, and feel the gradual darkness blend
Their august lineaments;—what time Haroun
Perambulated Bagdat, and none knew
He was the Caliph who knocked soberly
By Giafar's hand at their gates shut betimes;—
What time prince Assad sat on the high hill
'Neath the pomegranate-tree, long wearying
For his lost brother's step;—what time, as now,
Along our English sky, flame-furrows cleave
And break the quiet of the cold blue clouds,
And the first rays look in upon our roofs.

Let the day come or go; there is no let
Or hindrance to the indolent wilfulness
Of fantasy and dream-land. Place and time
And bodily weight are for the wakeful only.
Now they exist not: life is like that cloud,
Floating, poised happily in mid-air, bathed
In a sustaining halo, soft yet clear,
Voyaging on, though to no bourne; all heaven
Its own wide home alike, earth far below
Fading still further, further. Yet we see,
In fancy, its green fields, its towers, and towns
Smoking with life, its roads with traffic thronged
And tedious travellers within iron cars,
Its rivers with their ships, and laborers,

To whose raised eye, as, stretched upon the sward,
They may enjoy some interval of rest,
That little cloud appears no living thing,   70
Although it moves, and changes as it moves.
There is an old and memorable tale
Of some sound sleeper being borne away
By banded fairies in the mottled hour
Before the cockcrow, through unknown weird woods
And mighty forests, where the boughs and roots
Opened before him, closed behind;—thenceforth
A wise man lived he, all unchanged by years.
Perchance again these fairies may return,
And evermore shall I remain as now,   80
A dreamer half awake, a wandering cloud!

                    The spell
Of Merlin old that ministered to fate,
The tales of visiting ghosts, or fairy elves,
Or witchcraft, are no fables. But his task
Is ended with the night;—the thin white moon
Evades the eye, the sun breaks through the trees,
And the charmed wizard comes forth a mere man
From out his circle. Thus it is, whate'er
We know and understand hath lost the power   90
Over us;—we are then the master. Still
All Fancy's world is real; no diverse mark
Is on the stores of memory, whether gleaned
From childhood's early wonder at the charm
That bound the lady in the echoless cave
Where lay the sheath'd sword and the bugle horn,—
Or from the fullgrown intellect, that works
From age to age, exploring darkest truths,
With sympathy and knowledge in one yoke
Ploughing the harvest land.   100

                    The lark is up.
Piercing the dazzling sky beyond the search
Of the acutest love: enough for me

To hear its song: but now it dies away,
Leaving the chirping sparrow to attract
The listless ear,—a minstrel, sooth to say,
Nearly as good. And now a hum like that
Of swarming bees on meadow-flowers comes up.
Each hath its just and yet luxurious joy.
As if to live were to be blessed. The mild   110
Maternal influence of nature thus
Ennobles both the sentient and the dead:—
The human heart is as an altar wreathed.
On which old wine pours streaming o'er the leaves,
And down the symbol-carved sides. Behold!
Unbidden, yet most welcome, who be these?
The high-priests of this altar, poet-kings:—
Chaucer still young with silvery beard that seems
Worthy the adoration of a child;
And Spenser, perfect master, to whom all   120
Sweet graces ministered. The shut eye weaves
A picture;—the immortals pass along
Into the heaven, and others follow still,
Each on his own ray-path, till all the field
Is threaded with the foot-prints of the great.
And now the passengers are lost; long lines
Only are left, all intertwisted, dark
Upon a flood of light. . . . . I am awake!
I hear domestic voices on the stair.

Already hath the mower finished half   130
His summer day's ripe task; already hath
His scythe been whetted often; and the heaps
Behind him lie like ridges from the tide.
In sooth, it is high time to wave away
The cup of Comus, though with nectar filled,
And sweet as odours to the mariner
From lands unseen, across the wide blank sea.

SONNET*

When midst the summer-roses the warm bees
    Are swarming in the sun, and thou—so full
    Of innocent glee—dost with thy white hands pull
Pink scented apples from the garden trees
To fling at me, I catch them, on my knees,
Like those who gather'd manna; and I cull
Some hasty buds to pelt thee—white as wool
Lilies, or yellow jonquils, or heartsease;—
Then I can speak my love, ev'n tho' thy smiles
    Gush out among thy blushes, like a flock
Of bright birds from rose-bowers; but when thou'rt gone
    I have no speech,—no magic that beguiles,
    The stream of utterance from the harden'd rock:—
The dial cannot speak without the sun!

* Published in *The Germ*.

STARS AND MOON*

Beneath the stars and summer moon
　A pair of wedded lovers walk,
Upon the stars and summer moon
　They turn their happy eyes, and talk.

EDITH

"Those stars, that moon, for me they shine
　With lovely, but no startling light;
My joy is much, but not as thine,
　A joy that fills the pulse, like fright."

ALFRED

"My love, a darken'd conscience clothes
　The world in sackcloth; and, I fear,　　　　　10
The stain of life this new heart loathes,
　Still clouds my sight; but thine is clear.

"True vision is no startling boon
　To one in whom it always lies;
But if true sight of stars and moon
　Were strange to thee, it would surprise.

"Disease it is and dearth in me
　Which thou believest genius, wealth;
And that imagined want in thee
　Is riches and abundant health.　　　　　　20

"O, little merit I my bride!
　And therefore will I love her more;

* Published in *The Germ*.

Renewing, by her gentle side,
    Lost worth: let this thy smile restore!"

EDITH

"Ah, love! we both, with longing deep,
    Love words and actions kind, which are
More good for life than bread or sleep,
    More beautiful than Moon or Star.

FROM *The Child Jesus* *

THE CRUCIFIXION

Joseph had one ewe-sheep; and she brought forth,
Early one season, and before her time,
A weakly lamb. It chanced to be upon
Jesus' birthday, when he was eight years old.
So Mary said—"We'll name it after him,"—
(Because she ever thought to please her child)—
"And we will sign it with a small red cross
Upon the back, a mark to know it by."
And Jesus loved the lamb; and, as it grew
Spotless and pure and loving like himself,   10
White as the mother's milk it fed upon,
He gave not up his care, till it became
Of strength enough to browse; and then, because
Joseph had no land of his own, being poor,
He sent away the lamb to feed amongst
A neighbour's flock some distance from his home;
Where Jesus went to see it every day.
One late Spring eve, their daily work being done,
Mother and child, according to their wont,
Went, hand in hand, their chosen evening walk.   20
A pleasant wind rose from the sea, and blew
Light flakes of waving silver o'er the fields
Ready for mowing, and the golden West
Warmed half the sky: the low sun flickered through
The hedge-rows, as they passed; while hawthorn trees
Scattered their snowy leaves and scent around.
The sloping woods were rich in varied leaf,
And musical in murmur and in song.

Long ere they reached the field, the wistful lamb
    * Published in *The Germ*.

Saw them approach, and ran from side to side   30
The gate, pushing its eager face between
The lowest bars, and bleating for pure joy.
And Jesus, kneeling by it, fondled with
The little creature, that could scarce find how
To show its love enough; licking his hands,
Then, starting from him, gambolled back again,
And, with its white feet upon Jesus' knees,
Nestled its head by his: and, as the sun
Sank down behind them, broadening as it neared
The low horizon, Mary thought it seemed   40
To clothe them like a glory.—But her look
Grew thoughtful, and she said: "I had, last night,
A wandering dream. This brings it to my mind;
And I will tell it thee as we walk home.

"I dreamed a weary way I had to go
Alone, across an unknown land: such wastes
We sometimes see in visions of the night,
Barren and dimly lighted. There was not
A tree in sight, save on seared leafless trunk,
Like a rude cross; and, scattered here and there,   50
A shrivelled thistle grew: the grass was dead,
And the starved soil glared through its scanty tufts
In bare and chalky patches, cracked and hot,
Chafing my tired feet, that caught upon
Its parched surface; for a thirsty sun
Had sucked all moisture from the ground it burned,
And, red and glowing, stared upon me like
A furnace eye when all the flame is spent.
I felt it was a dream; and so I tried
To close my eyes, and shut it out from sight.   60
Then, sitting down, I hid my face; but this
Only increased the dread; and so I gazed
With open eyes into my dream again.
The mists had thickened, and had grown quite black
Over the sun; and darkness closed round me.
(Thy father said it thundered towards the morn.)
But soon, far off, I saw a dull green light

Break through the clouds, which fell across the earth,
Like death upon a bad man's upturned face.
Sudden it burst with fifty forked darts   70
In one white flash, so dazzling bright it seemed
To hide the landscape in one blaze of light.
When the loud crash that came down with it had
Rolled its long echo into stillness, through
The calm dark silence came a plaintive sound;
And, looking towards the tree, I saw that it
Was scorched with the lightning; and there stood
Close to its foot a solitary sheep
Bleating upon the edge of a deep pit,
Unseen till now, choked up with briars and thorns;   80
And into this a little snow white lamb,
Like to thine own, had fallen. It was dead
And cold, and must have lain there very long;
While, all the time, the mother had stood by,
Helpless, and moaning with a piteous bleat.
The lamb had struggled much to free itself,
For many cruel thorns had torn its head
And bleeding feet; and one had pierced its side,
From which flowed blood and water. Strange the things
We see in dreams, and hard to understand;—   90
For, stooping down to raise its lifeless head,
I thought it changed into the quiet face
Of my own child. Then I awoke, and saw
The dim moon shining through the watery clouds
On thee awake within thy little bed."

Then Jesus looking up, said quietly:
"We read that God will speak to those he loves
Sometimes in visions. He might speak to thee
Of things to come his mercy partly veils
From thee, my mother; or perhaps, the thought   100
Floated across thy mind of what we read
Aloud before we went to rest last night;—
I mean that passage in Isaias' book,
Which tells about the patient suffering lamb,
And which it seems that no one understands."

James Collinson/183

Then Mary bent her face to the child's brow,
And kissed him twice, and, parting back his hair,
Kissed him again. And Jesus felt her tears
Drop warm upon his cheek, and he looked sad
When silently he put his hand again 110
Within his mother's. As they came, they went,
Hand in hand homeward.
                And the child abode
With Mary and with Joseph, till the time
When all the things should be fulfilled in him
Which God had spoken by his prophets' mouth
Long since; and God was with him, and God's grace.

A SKETCH FROM NATURE *

The air blows pure, for twenty miles,
    Over this vast countrié:
Over hill and wood and vale, it goeth,
    Over steeple, and stack, and tree:
And there's not a bird on the wind but knoweth
    How sweet these meadows be.

The swallows are flying beside the wood,
    And the corbies are hoarsely crying;
And the sun at the end of the earth hath stood,
And, thorough the hedge and over the road,   10
    On the grassy slope is lying:
And the sheep are taking their supper-food
    While yet the rays are dying.

Sleepy shadows are filling the furrows,
    And giant-long shadows the trees are making;
And velvet soft are the woodland tufts,
And misty-gray the low-down crofts;
But the aspens there have gold-green tops,
    And the gold-green tops are shaking:
The spires are white in the sun's last light;—   20
And yet a moment ere he drops,
Gazes the sun on the golden slopes.

Two sheep, afar from fold,
    Are on the hill-side straying,
With backs all silver, breasts all gold:
    The merle is something saying,
Something very very sweet:—
    'The day—the day—the day is done:'
There answereth a single bleat—
The air is cold, the sky is dimming,   30
And clouds are long like fishes swimming.

    * Published in *The Germ*.

MY BEAUTIFUL LADY *

I love my lady; she is very fair;
Her brow is white, and bound by simple hair:
    Her spirit sits aloof, and high,
    Altho' it looks thro' her soft eye
    Sweetly and tenderly.

As a young forest, when the wind drives thro',
My life is stirred when she breaks on my view.
    Altho' her beauty has such power,
    Her soul is like the simple flower
    Trembling beneath a shower.   10

As bliss of saints, when dreaming of large wings,
The bloom around her fancied presence flings,
    I feast and wile her absence, by
    Pressing her choice hand passionately—
    Imagining her sigh.

My lady's voice, altho' so very mild,
Maketh me feel as strong wine would a child;
    My lady's touch, however slight,
    Moves all my senses with its might,
    Like to a sudden fright.   20

A hawk poised high in air, whose nerved wing-tips
Tremble with might suppressed, before he dips,—
    In vigilance, not more intense
    Than I; when her word's gentle sense
    Makes full-eyed my suspense.

Her mention of a thing—august or poor,
Makes it seem nobler than it was before:

    * Published in *The Germ.*

As where the sun strikes, life will gush,
And what is pale receive a flush,
Rich hues—a richer blush.   30

My lady's name, if I hear strangers use,—
Not meaning her—seems like a lax misuse.
    I love none but my lady's name;
    Rose, Maud, or Grace, are all the same,
    So blank, so very tame.

My lady walks as I have seen a swan
Swim thro' the water just where the sun shone.
    There ends of willow branches ride,
    Quivering with the current's glide,
    By the deep river-side.   40

Whene'er she moves there are fresh beauties stirred;
As the sunned bosom of a humming-bird
    At each pant shows some fiery hue,
    Burns gold, intensest green or blue:
    The same, yet ever new.

What time she walketh under flowering May,
I am quite sure the scented blossoms say,
    "O lady with the sunlit hair!
    Stay, and drink our odorous air—
    The incense that we bear: 50

"Your beauty, lady, we would ever shade;
Being near you, our sweetness might not fade."
    If trees could be broken-hearted,
    I am sure that the green sap smarted,
    When my lady parted.

This is why I thought weeds were beautiful;—
Because one day I saw my lady pull
    Some weeds up near a little brook,
    Which home most carefully she took,
    Then shut them in a book.   60

Thomas Woolner/187

A deer when startled by the stealthy ounce,—
A bird escaping from the falcon's trounce,
    Feels his heart swell as mine, when she
    Stands statelier, expecting me,
    Than tall white lilies be.

The first white flutter of her robe to trace,
Where binds and perfumed jasmine interlace,
    Expands my gaze triumphantly:
    Even such his gaze, who sees on high
    His flag, for victory.   70

We wander forth unconsciously, because
The azure beauty of the evening draws:
    When sober hues pervade the ground,
    And life in one vast hush seems drowned,
    Air stirs so little sound.

We thread a copse where frequent bramble spray
With loose obtrusion from the side roots stray,
    (Forcing sweet pauses on our walk):
    I'll lift one with my foot, and talk
    About its leaves and stalk.   80

Or may be that the prickles of some stem
Will hold a prisoner her long garment's hem;
    To disentangle it I kneel,
    Oft wounding more than I can heal;
    It makes her laugh, my zeal.

Then on before a thin-legged robin hops,
Or leaping on a twig, he pertly stops,
    Speaking a few clear notes, till nigh
    We draw, when quickly he will fly
    Into a bush close by.   90

A flock of goldfinches may stop their flight,
And wheeling round a birchen tree alight
    Deep in its glittering leaves, until

They see us, when their swift rise will
Startle a sudden thrill.

I recollect my lady in a wood,
Keeping her breath and peering—(firm she stood
    Her slim shape balanced on tiptoe—)
    Into a nest which lay below,
    Leaves shadowing her brow.   100

I recollect my lady asking me,
What that shap tapping in the wood might be?
    I told her blackbirds made it, which,
    For slimy morsels they count rich,
    Cracked the snail's curling niche:

She made no answer. When we reached the stone
Where the shell fragments on the grass were strewn,
    Close to the margin of a rill;
    "The air," she said, "seems damp and chill,
    We'll go home if you will."   110

"Make not my pathway dull so soon," I cried,
"See how those vast cloudpiles in sun-glow dyed,
    Roll out their splendor: while the breeze
    Lifts gold from leaf to leaf, as these
    Ash saplings move at ease."

Piercing the silence in our ears, a bird
Threw some notes up just then, and quickly stirred
    The covert birds that startled, sent
    Their music thro' the air; leaves lent
    Their rustling and blent,   120

Until the whole of the blue warmth was filled
So much with sun and sound, that the air thrilled.
    She gleamed, wrapt in the dying day's
    Glory: altho' she spoke no praise,
    I saw much in her gaze.

Thomas Woolner/189

Then, flushed with resolution, I told all;—
The mighty love I bore her,—how would pall
    My very breath of life, if she
    For ever breathed not hers with me;—
    Could I a cherub be,   130

How, idly hoping to enrich her grace,
I would snatch jewels from the orbs of space;—
    Then back thro' the vague distance beat,
    Glowing with joy her smile to meet,
    And heap them round her feet.

Her waist shook to my arm. She bowed her head,
Silent, with hands clasped and arms straightened:
    (Just then we both heard a church bell)
    O God! It is not right to tell:
    But I remember well   140

Each breast swelled with its pleasure, and her whole
Bosom grew heavy with love; the swift roll
    Of new sensations dimmed her eyes,
    Half closing them in ecstasies,
    Turned full against the skies.

The rest is gone; it seemed a whirling round—
No pressure of my feet upon the ground:
    But even when parted from her, bright
    Showed all; yea, to my throbbing sight
    The dark was starred with light.   150

OF MY LADY IN DEATH *

All seems a painted show. I look
    Up thro' the bloom that's shed
    By leaves above my head,
And feel the earnest life forsook
   * Published in *The Germ.*

All being, when she died:—
My heart halts, hot and dried
As the parched course where once a brook
    Thro' fresh growth used to flow,—
    Because her past is now
No more than stories in a printed book.   10

The grass has grown above that breast,
    Now cold and sadly still,
    My happy face felt thrill:—
Her mouth's mere tones so much expressed!
    Those lips are now close set,—
    Lips which my own have met;
Her eyelids by the earth are pressed;
    Damp earth weighs on her eyes;
    Damp earth shuts out the skies.
My lady rests her heavy, heavy rest.   20

To see her slim perfection sweep,
    Trembling impatiently,
    With eager gaze at me!
Her feet spared little things that creep:—
    "We've no more right," she'd say,
    In this the earth than they."
Some remember it but to weep.
    Her hand's slight weight was such,
    Care lightened with its touch;
My lady sleeps her heavy, heavy sleep.   30

My day-dreams hovered round her brow;
    Now o'er its perfect forms
    Go softly real worms.
Stern death, it was a cruel blow,
    To cut that sweet girl's life
    Sharply, as with a knife.
Cursed life that lets me live and grow,
    Just as a poisonous root,
    From which rank blossoms shoot;
My lady's laid so very, very low.   40

Dread power, grief cries aloud, "unjust,"—
    To let her young life play
    Its easy, natural way;
Then, with an unexpected thrust,
    Strike out the life you lent,
    Just when her feelings blent
With those around whom she saw trust
    Her willing power to bless,
    For their whole happiness;
My lady moulders into common dust.   50

Small birds twitter and peck the weeds
    That wave above her head,
    Shading her lowly bed:
Their brisk wings burst light globes of seeds,
    Scattering the downy pride
    Of dandelions, wide:
Speargrass stoops with watery beads:
    The weight from its fine tips
    Occasionally drips:
The bee drops in the mallow-bloom, and feeds.   60

About her window, at the dawn,
    From the vine's crooked boughs
    Birds chirupped an arouse:
Flies, buzzing, strengthened with the morn;—
    She'll not hear them again
    At random strike the pane:
No more upon the close-cut lawn,
    Her garment's sun-white hem
    Bend the prim daisy's stem,
In walking forth to view what flowers are born.   70

No more she'll watch the dark-green rings
    Stained quaintly on the lea,
    To image fairy glee;
While thro' dry grass a faint breeze sings,
    And swarms of insects revel
    Along the sultry level:—

No more will watch their brilliant wings,
    Now lightly dip, now soar,
    Then sink, and rise once more.
My lady's death makes dear these trivial things.   80

Within a huge tree's steady shade,
    When resting from our walk,
    How pleasant was her talk!
Elegant deer leaped o'er the glade,
    Or stood with wide bright eyes,
    Staring a short surprise:
Outside the shadow cows were laid,
    Chewing with drowsy eye
    Their cuds complacently:
Dim for sunshine drew near a milking-maid.   90

Rooks cawed and labored thro' the heat;
    Each wing-flap seemed to make
    Their weary bodies ache:
The swallows, tho' so very fleet,
    Made breathless pauses there
    At something in the air:—
All disappeared: our pulses beat
    Distincter throbs: then each
    Turned and kissed, without speech,—
She trembling, from her mouth down to her feet.   100

My head sank on her bosom's heave,
    So close to the soft skin
    I heard the life within.
My forehead felt her coolly breathe,
    As with her breath it rose:
    To perfect my repose
Her two arms clasped my neck. The eve
    Spread silently around,
    A hush along the ground,
And all sound with the sunlight seemed to leave.   110

By my still gaze she must have known

The mighty bliss that filled
My whole soul, for she thrilled,
Drooping her face, flushed, on my own;
I felt that it was such
By its light warmth of touch,
My lady was with me alone:
That vague sensation brought
More real joy than thought.
I am without her now, truly alone. 120

We had no heed of time: the cause
Was that our minds were quite
Absorbed in our delight,
Silently blessed. Such stillness awes,
And stops with doubt, the breath,
Like the mute doom of death.
I felt Time's instantaneous pause;
An instant, on my eye
Flashed all Eternity:—
I started, as if clutched by wild beasts' claws, 130

Awakened from some dizzy swoon:
I felt strange vacant fears,
With singings in my ears,
And wondered that the pallid moon
Swung round the dome of night
With such tremendous might.
A sweetness, like the air of June,
Next paled me with suspense,
A weight of clinging sense—
Some hidden evil would burst on me soon. 140

My lady's love has passed away,
To know that it is so
To me is living woe.
That body lies in cold decay,
Which held the vital soul
When she was my life's soul.
Bitter mockery it was to say—

"Our souls are as the same:"
My words now sting like shame;
Her spirit went, and mine did not obey.   150

It was as if a fiery dart
    Passed seething thro' my brain
    When I beheld her lain
There whence in life she did not part.
    Her beauty by degrees,
    Sank, sharpened with disease:
The heavy sinking at her heart
    Sucked hollows in her cheek,
    And made her eyelids weak,
Tho' oft they'd open wide with sudden start.   160

The deathly power in silence drew
    My lady's life away.
    I watched, dumb with dismay,
The shock of thrills that quivered thro'
    And tightened every limb:
    For grief my eyes grew dim;
More near, more near, the moment grew.
    O horrible suspense!
    O giddy impotence!
I saw her fingers lax, and change their hue.   170

Her gaze, grown large with fate, was cast
    Where my mute agonies
    Made more sad her sad eyes:
Her breath caught with short plucks and fast:—
    Then one hot choking strain.
    She never breathed again:
I had the look which was her last:
    Even after breath was gone,
    Her love one moment shone,—
Then slowly closed, and hope for ever passed.   180

Silence seemed to start in space
    When first the bell's harsh toll

Rang for my lady's soul.
Vitality was hell; her grace
    The shadow of a dream:
    Things then did scarcely seem:
Oblivion's stroke fell like a mace:
        As a tree that's just hewn
        I dropped, in a dead swoon,
And lay a long time cold upon my face.   190

Earth had one quarter turned before
    My miserable fate
    Pressed on with its whole weight.
My sense came back; and, shivering o'er,
    I felt a pain to bear
    The sun's keen cruel glare;
It seemed not warm as heretofore.
        Oh, never more its rays
        Will satisfy my gaze.
No more; no more; oh, never any more.   200

CADENCES

I

(MINOR)

The ancient memories buried lie,
   And the olden fancies pass;
The old sweet flower-thoughts wither and fly,
And die as the April cowslips die,
   That scatter the bloomy grass.

All dead, my dear! And the flowers are dead,
   And the happy blossoming spring;
The winter comes with its iron tread,
The fields with the dying sun are red,
   And the birds have ceas'd to sing.   **10**

I trace the steps on the wasted strand
   Of the vanish'd springtime's feet:
Wither'd and dead is our Fairyland,
For Love and Death go hand in hand
   Go hand in hand, my sweet!

II

(MAJOR)

Oh, what shall be the burden of our rhyme,
And what shall be our ditty when the blossom's on the lime?
Our lips have fed on winter and on weariness too long:
We will hail the royal summer with a golden-footed song!

   O lady of my summer and my spring,   **20**
We shall hear the blackbird whistle and the brown
   sweet throstle sing,

And the low clear noise of waters running softly by our feet,
When the sights and sounds of summer in the green clear
        fields are sweet.

    We shall see the roses blowing in the green,
The pink-lipp'd roses kissing in the golden summer sheen;
We shall see the fields flower thick with stars and bells of
        summer gold,
And the poppies burn out red and sweet across the
        corn-crown'd wold.

    The time shall be for pleasure, not for pain;
There shall come no ghost of grieving for the past betwixt
        us twain;
But in the time of roses our lives shall grow together,   30
And our love be as the love of gods in the blue
        Olympic weather.

SIBYL

This is the glamour of the world antique:
The thyme-scents of Hymettus fill the air,
And in the grass narcissus-cups are fair.
The full brook wanders through the ferns to seek
The amber haunts of bees; and on the peak
Of the soft hill, against the gold-marged sky,
She stands, a dream from out the days gone by.
Entreat her not. Indeed, she will not speak!
Her eyes are full of dreams; and in her ears
There is the rustle of immortal wings;
And ever and anon the slow breeze bears
The mystic murmur of the songs she sings.
Entreat her not: she sees thee not, nor hears
Aught but the sights and sounds of bygone springs.

A MODERN IDYL *

Pride clings to age, for few and withered powers,
  Which fall on youth in pleaures manifold,
Like some bright dancer with a crowd of flowers
  And scented presents more than she can hold:

"Or as it were a child beneath a tree,
  Who in his healthy joy holds hand and cap
Beneath the shaken boughs, and eagerly
  Expects the fruit to fall into his lap."

So thought I while my cousin sat alone,
Moving with many leaves in under tone,   10
And, sheened as snow lit by a pale moonlight,
Her childish dress struck clearly on the sight:
That, as the lilies growing by her side
Casting their silver radiance forth with pride,
She seemed to dart an arrowy halo round,
Brightening the spring time trees, brightening the ground;
And beauty, like keen lustre from a star,
Glorified all the garden near and far.
The sunlight smote the grey and mossy wall
Where, 'mid the leaves, the peaches one and all,   20
Most like twin cherubim entranced above,
Leaned their soft cheeks together, pressed in love.

As the child sat, the tendrils shook round her;
And, blended tenderly in middle air,
Gleamed the long orchard through the ivied gate:
And slanting sunbeams made the heart elate,
Startling it into gladness like the sound,—
Which echo childlike mimicks faintly round
Blending it with the lull of some far flood,—

  * Published in *The Germ*.

Of one long shout heard in a quiet wood.   30
A gurgling laugh far off the fountain sent,
As if the mermaid shape that in it bent
Spoke with subdued and faintest melody:
And birds sang their whole hearts spontaneously.

When from your books released, pass here your hours,
Dear child, the sweet companion of these flowers,
These poplars, scented shrubs, and blossomed boughs
Of fruit-trees, where the noisy sparrows house,
Shaking from off the leaves the beaded dew.
Now while the air is warm, the heavens blue,   40
Give full abandonment to all your gay
Swift childlike impulses in rompish play;—
The while your sisters in shrill laughter shout,
Whirling above the leaves and round about,—
Until at length it drops behind the wall,—
With awkward jerks, the particoloured ball:
Winning a smile even from the stooping age
Of that old matron leaning on her page,
Who in the orchard takes a stroll or two,
Watching you closely yet unseen by you.   50

Then, tired of gambols, turn into the dark
Fir-skirted margins of your father's park;
And watch the moving shadows, as you pass,
Trace their dim network on the tufted grass,
And how on birch-trunks smooth and branches old,
The velvet moss bursts out in green and gold,
Like the rich lustre full and manifold
On breasts of birds that star the curtained gloom
From their glass cases in the drawing room.
Mark the spring leafage bend its tender spray   60
Gracefully on the sky's aërial grey;
And listen how the birds so voluble
Sing joyful paeans winding to a swell,
And how the wind, fitful and mournful, grieves
In gusty whirls among the dry red leaves;

And watch the minnows in the water cool,
And floating insects wrinkling all the pool.

So in your ramblings bend your earnest eyes.
   High thoughts and feelings will come unto you,—
   Gladness will fall upon your heart like dew,—   70
Because you love the earth and love the skies.

Fair pearl, the pride of all our family:
   Girt with the plentitude of joys so strong,
   Fashion and custom dull can do no wrong:
Nestling your young face thus on Nature's knee.

THE FAIR MAID AND THE SUN

O sons of men, that toil, and love with tears!

Know ye, O sons of men, the maid who dwells
Between the two seas at the Dardanelles?
   Her face hath charm'd away the change of years,
And all the world is filled with her spells.

No task is hers forever, but the play
Of setting forth her beauty day by day:
   There in your midst, O sons of men that toil,
She laughs the long eternity away.

The chains about her neck are many pearl'd,   10
Rare gems are those round which her hair is curl'd;
   She hath all flesh for captive, and for spoil,
The fruit of all the labor of the world.

She getteth up and maketh herself bare,
And letteth down the wonder of her hair
   Before the sun; the heavy golden locks
Fall in the hollow of her shoulders fair.

She taketh from the lands, as she may please,
All jewels, and all corals from the seas;
   She layeth them in rows upon the rocks;   20
Laugheth, and bringeth fairer ones than these.

Five are the goodly necklaces that deck
The place between her bosom and her neck;
   She passeth many a bracelet o'er her hands;
And, seeing she is white without a fleck,

And seeing she is fairer than the tide,

And of a beauty no man can abide,
　Proudly she standeth as a goddess stands,
And mocketh at the sun and sea for pride:

And to the sea she saith: "O silver sea,　　　　30
Fair art thou, but thou art not fair like me;
　Open thy white-tooth'd, dimpled mouths and try;
They laugh not the soft way I laugh at thee."

And to the sun she saith: "O golden sun,
Fierce is thy burning till the day is done!
　But thou shalt burn mere grass and leaves, while I
Shall burn the hearts of men up every one."

O fair and dreadful is the maid who dwells
Between the two seas at the Dardanelles,—
　As fair and dread as in the ancient years;　　40
And still the world is filled with her spells.

O sons of men, that toil, and love with tears!

HAS SUMMER COME WITHOUT THE ROSE?

Has summer come without the rose,
　Or left the bird behind?
Is the blue changed above thee,
　O world! or am I blind?
Will you change every flower that grows,
　Or only change this spot,
Where she who said, I love thee,
　Now says, I love thee not?

The skies seem'd true above thee,
　The rose true on the tree;　　　　　　　　10
The bird seem'd true the summer through,
　But all prov'd false to me.
World, is there one good thing in you,

Life, love, or death—or what?
Since lips that sang, I love thee,
    Have said, I love thee not?

I think the sun's kiss will scarce fall
    Into one flower's gold cup;
I think the bird will miss me,
    And give the summer up.   20
O sweet place, desolate in tall
    Wild grass, have you forgot
How her lips lov'd to kiss me,
    Now that they kiss me not?

Be false or fair above me;
    Come back with any face,
Summer!—do I care what you do?
    You cannot change one place,—
The grass, the leaves, the earth, the dew,
    The grave I make the spot,—   30
Here, where she used to love me,
    Here, where she loves me not.

THE LOVE OF BEAUTY *

John Boccaccio, love's own squire, deep sworn
  In service to all beauty, joy, and rest,—
  When first the love-earned royal Mary press'd,
To her smooth cheek, his pale brows, passion-worn,—
'Tis said, he, by her grace nigh frenzied, torn
  By longings unattainable, address'd
  To his chief friend most strange misgivings, lest
Some madness in his brain had thence been born.
The artist-mind alone can feel his meaning:—
  Such as have watched the battle-rank'd array
Of sunset, or the face of girlhood seen in
  Line-blending twilight, with sick hope. Oh! they
May feed desire on some fond bosom leaning:
  But where shall such their thirst of Nature stay?

FOR THE PICTURE, "THE LAST OF ENGLAND" [1]

"The last of England! O'er the sea, my dear,
Our homes to seek amid Australian fields,
Us, not our million-acred island yields
The space to dwell in. Thrust out! Forced to hear
Low ribaldry from sots, and share rough cheer
With rudely-nurtur'd men. The hope youth builds
Of fair renown, barter'd for that which shields
Only the back, and half-form'd lands that rear
The dust-storm blistering up the grasses wild.
There learning skills not, nor the poet's dream,
Nor aught so lov'd as children shall we see."
She grips his listless hand and clasps her child,
Through rainbow tears she sees a sunnier gleam,
She cannot see a void, where he will be.

  * Published in *The Germ*.
  [1] "The Last of England" was painted by Brown himself;
it shows a man and woman sitting by the rail of a ship, staring
toward the receding shore.

THE FAIRIES

A CHILD'S SONG

Up the airy mountain,
   Down the rushy glen,
We daren't go a-hunting
   For fear of little men;
Wee folk, good folk,
   Trooping all together;
Green jacket, red cap,
   And white owl's feather!
Down along the rocky shore
   Some make their home,—   10
They live on crispy pancakes
   Of yellow tide-foam;
Some in the reeds
   Of the black mountain-lake,
With frogs for their watch-dogs,
   All night awake.

High on the hill-top
   The old King sits;
He is now so old and gray
   He's nigh lost his wits.   20
With a bridge of white mist
   Columbkill he crosses,
On his stately journeys
   From Slieveleague to Rosses;
Or going up with music
   On cold starry nights,
To sup with the Queen
   Of the gay Northern Lights.

They stole little Bridget

For seven years long;
When she came down again
  Her friends were all gone.
They took her lightly back,
  Between the night and morrow,
They thought that she was fast asleep,
  But she was dead with sorrow.
They have kept her ever since
  Deep within the lakes,
On a bed of flag-leaves,
  Watching till she wakes.

By the craggy hill-side,
  Through the mosses bare,
They have planted thorn-trees
  For pleasure here and there.
Is any man so daring
  As dig one up in spite,
He shall find the thornies set
  In his bed at night.

Up the airy mountain,
  Down the rushy glen,
We daren't go a-hunting
  For fear of little men;
Wee folk, good folk,
  Trooping all together;
Green jacket, red cap,
  And white owl's feather!

THE SAILOR

A ROMAIC BALLAD [1]

Thou that hast a daughter
  For one to woo and wed,

[1] Romaic is the modern Greek language.

Give her to a husband
  With snow upon his head;
Oh, give her to an old man,
  Though little joy it be,
Before the best young sailor
  That sails upon the sea!

How luckless is the sailor
  When sick and like to die;   10
He sees no tender mother,
  No sweetheart standing by.
Only the captain speaks to him,—
  Stand up, stand up, young man,
And steer the ship to haven,
  As none beside thee can.

Thou say'st to me, "Stand up, stand up:"
  I say to thee, take hold,
Lift me a little from the deck,
  My hands and feet are cold.   20
And let my head, I pray thee,
  With handkerchiefs be bound;
There, take my love's gold handkerchief,
  And tie it tightly round.

Now bring the chart, the doleful chart;
  See, where these mountains meet—
The clouds are thick around their head,
  The mists around their feet;
Cast anchor here; 't is deep and safe
  Within the rocky cleft;   30
The little anchor on the right,
  The great one on the left.

And now to thee, O captain,
  Most earnestly I pray,
That they may never bury me
  In church or cloister gray;
But on the windy sea-beach,

At the ending of the land,
All on the surfy sea-beach,
   Deep down into the sand.

For there will come the sailors,
   Their voices I shall hear,
And at casting of the anchor
   The yo-ho loud and clear;
And at hauling of the anchor
   The yo-ho and the cheer,—
Farewell, my love, for to thy bay
   I nevermore may steer!

A DREAM

I heard the dogs howl in the moonlight night;
I went to the window to see the sight;
All the Dead that ever I knew
Going one by one and two by two.

On they pass'd, and on they pass'd;
Townsfellows all, from first to last;
Born in the moonlight of the lane,
Quench'd in the heavy shadow again.

Schoolmates, marching as when we play'd
At soldiers once—but now more staid;
Those were the strangest sight to me
Who were drown'd, I knew, in the awful sea.

Straight and handsome folk; bent and weak, too;
Some that I lov'd, and gasp'd to speak to;
Some but a day in their churchyard bed;
Some that I had not known were dead.

A long, long crowd—where each seem'd lonely,
Yet of them all there was one, one only,

Raised a head or look'd my way:
She linger'd a moment,—she might not stay.   20

How long since I saw that fair pale face!
Ah! Mother dear! might I only place
My head on thy breast, a moment to rest,
While thy hand on my tearful cheek were prest!

On, on, a moving bridge they made
Across the moon-stream, from shade to shade,
Young and old, women and men;
Many long-forgot, but remember'd then.

And first there came a bitter laughter;
A sound of tears the moment after;   30
And then a music so lofty and gay,
That every morning, day by day,
I strive to recall it if I may.

THE BREADTH AND BEAUTY OF THE
SPACIOUS NIGHT

The breadth and beauty of the spacious night
    Brimmed with white moonlight, swept by winds that
    blew
  The flying sea-spray up to where we two
Sat all alone, made one in Love's delight,—
The sanctity of sunsets palely bright;
  Autumnal woods, seen 'neath meek skies of blue,
  Old cities that God's silent peace stole through,—
These of our love were very sound and sight.

The strain of labor; the bewildering din
  Of thundering wheels; the bells' discordant chime;
  The sacredness of art; the spell of rhyme,—
These, too, with our dear love were woven in,
  That so, when parted, all things might recall
  The sacred love that had its part in all.

LOVE ASLEEP

I found Love sleeping in a place of shade,
    And as in some sweet dream the sweet lips smiled;
  Yea, seemed he as a lovely, sleeping child.
Soft kisses on his full, red lips I laid,
And with red roses did his tresses braid;
  Then pure, white lilies on his breast I piled,
  And fettered him with woodbine sweet and wild,
And fragrant armlets for his arms I made.

But while I, leaning, yearned across his breast,
  Upright he sprang, and from swift hand, alert,

Sent forth a shaft that lodged within my heart.
Ah, had I never played with Love at rest,
    He had not wakened, had not cast his dart,
And I had lived who die now of this hurt.

THE ROSE AND THE WIND

The Rose

When, think you, comes the Wind,
The Wind that kisses me and is so kind?
Lo, how the Lily sleeps! her sleep is light;
Would I were like the Lily, pale and white!
Will the Wind come?

The Beech

              Perchance for you too soon.

The Rose

If not, how could I live until the noon;
What, think you, Beech-tree, makes the Wind delay?
Why comes he not at breaking of the day?

The Beech

Hush, child, and, like the Lily, go to sleep.   10

The Rose

You know I cannot.

The Beech

            Nay, then, do not weep.

(*After a pause*)

Your lover comes, be happy now, O Rose!
He softly through my bending branches goes.
Soon he shall come, and you shall feel his kiss.

212/*Philip Bourke Marston*

The Rose

Already my flush'd heart grows faint with bliss;
Love, I have long'd for you through all the night.

The Wind

And I to kiss your petals warm and bright.

The Rose

Laugh round me, Love, and kiss me; it is well.
Nay, have no fear, the Lily will not tell.   20

MORNING

The Rose

'Twas dawn when first you came; and now the sun
Shines brightly and the dews of dawn are done.
'Tis well you take me so in your embrace;
But lay me back again into my place,
For I am worn, perhaps with bliss extreme.

The Wind

Nay, you must wake, Love, from this chillish dream.

The Rose

'Tis you, Love, who seem changed; your laugh is loud,
And 'neath your stormy kiss my head is bow'd.
O Love, O Wind, a space will you not spare?

The Wind

Not while your petals are so soft and fair.   30

The Rose

My buds are blind with leaves, they cannot see,
O Love, O Wind, will you not pity me?

EVENING

The Beech

O Wind, a word with you before you pass;

What did you to the Rose that on the grass
Broken she lies and pale, who lov'd you so?

The Wind

Roses must live and love, and winds must blow.

LOVE'S LOST PLEASURE-HOUSE

Love built for himself a Pleasure-House,—
   A Pleasure-House fair to see:
The roof was gold, and the walls thereof
   Were delicate ivory.

Violet crystal the windows were,
   All gleaming and fair to see;
Pillars of rose-stained marble up-bore
   That house where men longed to be.

Violet, golden, and white and rose,
   That Pleasure-House fair to see   10
Did show to all; and they gave Love thanks
   For work of such mastery.

Love turned away from his Pleasure-House,
   And stood by the salt, deep sea:
He looked therein, and he flung therein
   Of his treasure the only key.

Now never a man till time be done
   That Pleasure-House fair to see
Shall fill with music and merriment,
   Or praise it on bended knee.   20

REQUIEM

Wither'd pansies faint and sweet,
  O'er his breast in silence shed,
Faded lilies o'er his feet,
  Waning roses round his head,
Where in dreamless sleep he lies—
Folded palms and sealed eyes—
  Young Love, within my bosom—dead.

Young Love that was so fond, so fair,
  With his mouth of rosy red,
Argent wing and golden hair,   10
  And those blue eyen, glory-fed
From some fount of splendor, far
Beyond or moon or sun or star—
  And can it be that he is dead?

Ay! his breast is cold as snow:
  Pulse and breath forever fled;
If I kiss'd him ever so,
  To my kiss he were as lead;
If I clipp'd him as of yore
He would answer me no more   20
  With lip or hand—for he is dead.

But breathe no futile sigh; no tear
  Smirch his pure and lonely bed.
Let no foolish cippus rear
  Its weight above him. Only spread
Rose, lily, pale forget-me-not,
And pansies round the silent spot
  Where in his youth he lieth—dead.

WITH THE SUNSHINE AND THE SWALLOWS

With the sunshine and the swallows and the flowers,
   She is coming, my belovèd, o'er the sea!
And I sit alone and count the weary hours,
   Till she cometh in her beauty back to me;
     And my heart will not be quiet,
     But, in a "purple riot,"
     Keeps ever madly beating
     At the thought of that sweet meeting,
When she cometh with the summer o'er the sea;
     All the sweetness of the south   10
     On the roses of her mouth,
     All the fervour of its skies
     In her gentle northern eyes,
As she cometh, my belovèd, home to me!

No more, o' nights, the shivering north complains,
   But blithe birds twitter in the crimson dawn;
No more the fairy frost-flowers fret the panes,
   But snowdrops gleam by garden-path and lawn;
     And at times a white cloud wingeth
     From the southland up, and bringeth   20
     A warm wind, odour-laden,
     From the bowers of that fair Aden
Where she lingers by the blue Tyrrhenian Sea;
     And I turn my lips to meet
     Its kisses faint and sweet;
     For I know from hers they've brought
     The message, rapture-fraught:
"I am coming, love, with summer, home to thee!"

William Allingham (1824–1889): an associate of the Pre-Raphaelites, he was influenced by D. G. Rossetti, with whom he later quarreled. He earned his living as a civil servant and as a hack journalist. His poetry was published between 1850 and 1884.

Ford Maddox Brown (1821–1893): Brown was never an "official" member of the P.R.B., but he was a close and influential associate. He was born in Calais, France, and studied on the Continent, where he saw the work of the "Nazarenes" in Rome. He wrote little poetry, and is known chiefly as a painter.

Calder Campbell (c. 1790–?): Campbell, who published a poem in *The Germ*, was influential in focusing Pre-Raphaelite admiration upon the poetry of Keats. He was a friend and mentor of D. G. Rossetti.

James Collinson (1825–1881): Collinson contributed to *The Germ*, and may have been the lover of Christina Rossetti (though recent studies cite William Bell Scott as the object of her affection: see L. M. Packer, *Christina Rossetti*, Berkeley, Calif., 1963). He was a member of the P.R.B.

Walter H. Deverell (1828–1854): painter and poet, a contributor to *The Germ*.

Philip Bourke Marston (1850–1887): Marston was blind, and seems to have led an altogether wretched life, his family and friends dying off one by one until he finished his own days in straitened circumstances. Swinburne said of him that he had "an affectionate nature, and the most beautiful face I ever saw on a man."

William Morris (1834–1896): one of the giants in nineteenth-century art, Morris was a painter, poet, engraver, and designer—to name only a few of his talents. He fell under the spell of Rossetti but later quarreled with him. In politics he was a liberal, a "socialist," and his broad interests led him to studies of the Icelandic sagas (which he translated) and Norse mythology. His Kelmscott Press was perhaps the greatest press (in terms of quality) in Victorian England.

Arthur O'Shaughnessy (1844–1881): a London-born poet and an intimate friend of most of the Pre-Raphaelites. He was very much interested in French literature, and did many translations of French poetry, including the lays of Marie de France. He was the brother-in-law of Philip Bourke Marston.

Coventry Patmore (1823–1896): Patmore was a Pre-Raphaelite more by association than by inclination. He suggested to Ruskin that he (Ruskin) should defend the paintings of the P.R.B., and thus played a role in their eventual success. He contributed to *The Germ*. By the 1860's, Patmore was no longer associated with Pre-Raphaelitism.

Joseph Noël Paton (1821–1901): a painter and sculptor born in Scotland, Paton was eventually knighted (1867). His poetry shows an obvious debt to the Pre-Raphaelites.

John Payne (1842–1916): Rossetti and Swinburne were early admirers of Payne's poetry. Payne had abundant ego, and felt throughout most of his long life that he had been over-looked owing to the jealousy of other poets.

Christina Rossetti (1830–1894): The sister of Dante Gabriel and William Michael Rossetti, Christina served as the model for many paintings by her brother Dante. Her "Goblin Market" was the first well-known Pre-Raphaelite poem. Her poor health seems to have predisposed her toward the melancholy view that is evident in much of her poetry.

Dante Gabriel Rossetti (1828–1882): the most famous Pre-Raphaelite. Rossetti was a student of Dante Alighieri, and did many translations of his works. He was a painter as well as a poet, and it is his paintings that are probably the best known Pre-Raphaelite works today. He married Elizabeth Siddal after being deeply in love with her for many years; when she died in 1862 he was deeply stricken, and continued to paint her portrait for many years, although other women entered his life. Rossetti's magnetic personality seems to have been the unifying force of the P.R.B. and, in fact, of the whole Pre-Raphaelite movement.

William Michael Rossetti (1829–1919): the recorder of life among the P.R.B. members, he did not paint, although he did write poetry, several examples of which were printed in *The Germ*. He was the editor of the Rossetti family papers and a frequent contributor to art and literary journals throughout his life.

William Bell Scott (1811–1890): born in Scotland, Scott was deeply influenced by D. G. Rossetti, Morris, and Swinburne. He contributed to *The Germ*.

Algernon Charles Swinburne (1837–1909): Swinburne had the most colorful personality of all the Pre-Raphaelites. His flamboyance and peculiar appearance made him the object of much contemporary satiric humor. Swinburne was deeply influenced by D. G. Rossetti early in his career as a poet, although he felt that by 1861 he was no longer affected by Pre-Raphaelitism. He was at the center of the "Fleshly School of Poetry" battle (see Introduction).

J. L. Tupper (?–1879): Tupper was deeply influenced by D. G. Rossetti. He published a poem in *The Germ*. His works were edited by William Michael Rossetti in 1897. He was best known as a sculptor.

Thomas Woolner (1825–1892): Woolner was a sculptor, and did not feel that he had a very great poetic talent, although his contributions to *The Germ* (see pages 186-196) are imaginative. He was a member of the P.R.B.

I. PRIMARY SOURCES

A. BOOKS

Allingham, William. *Poems.* Selected and Arranged by Helen Allingham (Golden Treasury Series). London: Macmillan, 1912.

Marston, Philip Bourke. *The Collected Poems: Comprising "Song-Tide," "All in All," "Wind-Voices," "A Last Harvest," and "Aftermath."* Edited with a biographical sketch by Louise Chandler Moulton. London: Ward, 1892.

Morris, William. *The Defence of Guenevere and Other Poems.* London: Bell and Daldy, 1858.

O'Shaughnessy, Arthur W. E. *Poems.* Selected and Edited by William Alexander Percy. New Haven: Yale University Press, 1923.

Page, Frederick, ed. *The Poems of Coventry Patmore; with an Introduction.* London: Oxford University Press, 1949.

Rossetti, Christina Georgina. *The Poetical Works.* With Memoir and Notes by William M. Rossetti. London: Macmillan, 1904.

The Poems of Dante Gabriel Rossetti with Illustrations from His Own Pictures and Designs. Edited with an Introduction and Notes by William M. Rossetti. 2 vols. London: Ellis, 1904.

Rossetti, William Michael. *Democratic Sonnets* (The Contemporary Poets Series). 2 vols. London: Rivers, 1907.

Rossetti, William Michael, ed. *Ruskin: Rossetti, Pre-Raphaelitism Papers 1854 to 1862.* London: Allen, 1899.

Stedman, Edmund C., ed. *A Victorian Anthology.* Boston: Houghton, 1895.

Swinburne, Algernon Charles. *The Complete Works* (The Bonchurch Edition), Edited by Sir Edmund Gosse and Thomas J. Wise. 20 vols. London: Heinemann, 1927.

Woolner, Thomas. *Poems. Nelly Dale. Children.* London: Bell, 1887.

Yeats, William Butler. *The Autobiography of William Butler Yeats.* New York: Doubleday Anchor Books, 1958.

Yeats, William Butler. *The Collected Poems of W. B. Yeats.*
New York: Macmillan, 1953.

B. MAGAZINES

*The Germ: Thoughts Towards Nature in Poetry, Literature,
and Art.* Numbers 1 and 2, January and February, 1850.
Continued as *Art and Poetry, Being Thoughts Towards
Nature, Conducted Principally by Artists.* Numbers 3
and 4, March and April [dated May], 1850.
*The Oxford and Cambridge Magazine for 1856: Conducted
by Members of the Two Universities,* edited by William
Fulford. Oxford: Numbers 1–12, January to December,
1856.

II. SECONDARY SOURCES

A. BOOKS

Beers, Henry Augustin. "The Pre-Raphaelites," *A History of
English Romanticism in the Nineteenth Century.* New
York: Holt, 1901.
Buchanan, Robert. " 'The House of Life,' etc., Re-examined,"
*The Fleshly School of Poetry and Other Phenomenons
of the Day.* London: Strahan, 1872.
Buckley, Jerome H. "The Fear of Art," *The Victorian Temper: A Study in Literary Culture.* Cambridge, Mass.:
Harvard University Press, 1951.
Dickason, David H. *The Daring Young Men: The Story of
the American Pre-Raphaelites.* Bloomington: Indiana
University Press, 1953.
Evans, B. Ifor. "Minor Pre-Raphaelite Poets: William Bell
Scott; William Allingham; Thomas Woolner; Arthur
O'Shaughnessy; John Payne; Philip Bourke Marston;
William Sharp (Fiona Macleod)," *English Poetry in
the Later Nineteenth Century.* London: Methuen, 1933.
Fairchild, Hoxie Neale. "Dante Gabriel Rossetti," *Religious
Trends in English Poetry.* Vol. IV. 1830–1880. *Christianity and Romanticism in the Victorian Era.* New
York: Columbia University Press, 1957.
Ford, George H. "Morris, Swinburne, and Some Others,"
*Keats, and the Victorians: A Study of His Influence and
Rise to Fame, 1821–1895* (Yale Studies in English, Vol.
101). New Haven: Yale University Press, 1944 .

Forman, H. Buxton. "The Pre-Raphaelite Group," *Our Liv-ing Poets: An Essay in Criticism*. London: Tinsl...

Fredeman, William E. *Pre-Raphaelitism: A Bi... Study*. Cambridge, Mass.: Harvard Unive... 1965.

Galletti, Alfredo. "Dante Gabriele Rossetti e ... raffaellita," *Studi di letterature straniere*. ... telli Drucker, 1903.

Groom, Bernard. "Rossetti, Morris, and S... *Diction of Poetry from Spenser to Brid...* versity Press, 1955.

Hamilton, Walter. *The Aesthetic Moveme...* ed. London: Reeves and Turner, 18...

Hearn, Lafcadio. "Studies on Rossetti," ... *Other Poets: Lectures*. Selected ar... troduction by John Erskine. Ne... 1922.

Hueffer, Ford Maddox. *The Pre-...* London: Duckworth, 1907.

Hunt, William Holman. *Pre-R...* *Raphaelite Brotherhood.* 2... 1905–1906.

Jones, Howard Mumford, *et. ...* ment," *Syllabus and Bi...* ture. 2 vols. Ann Arbor:...

Jones, Howard Mumford. "...* torian Poets: A Guide...* E. Faverty. Cambridg... 1956.

Le Gallienne, Richard. "Arthur ... *tive Reviews.* Vol. II. London: Jo...

———. "Philip Bourke Marston: Last Harve... *tive Reviews.* Vol. I. London: John Lane, 18...

Le Roy, G. C. "Dante Gabriel Rossetti," *Perplexed Prophe...* Philadelphia: University of Pennsylvania Press, for Tem-ple University Publications, 1953.

Mégroz, R. L. "Pre-Raphaelite Poetry," *Modern English Poetry, 1882–1932*. London: Nicholson, 1933.

Packer, Lona Mosk. *Christina Rossetti*. Berkeley: University of California Press, 1963.

Pater, Walter Horatio. "Dante Gabriel Rossetti," in *The English Poets: Selections with Critical Introductions by*

Robson, W. W. "Pre-Raphaelite Poetry," in *From Dickens to Hardy*. *The Pelican Guide to English Literature. VI*, edited by Boris Ford. London: Penguin Books, 1958.

Walker, Hugh. "The Pre-Raphaelites," *The Literature of the Victorian Era*. Cambridge University Press, 1910; rev. ed., 1921.

Weatherby, David. "Problems of Form and Content in the Poetry of Dante Gabriel Rossetti," *Victorian Poetry...* (Winter 1964), 11–19.

Mégro... and Hi... 1928), 4–1...

Packer, Lona Mosk. ... setti's *Goblin Market,* ... guage Association, LXXIII (...